THALASSA: A THEORY OF GENITALITY

THALASSA

A THEORY OF GENITALITY

BY SANDOR FERENCZI , M.D.

TRANSLATED BY

HENRY ALDEN BUNKER, M.D.

KARNAC

LONDON   NEW YORK

Published in 1938 by The Psychoanalytic Quarterly, New York
Reprinted 1989 with the permission of Dr Judith Dupont
and by arrangement with Mark Paterson by
H. Karnac (Books) Ltd,
6 Pembroke Buildings
London NW10 6RE

This edition reprinted in 2005

Authorized Translation from the original German version entitled
Versuch einer Genitaltheorie
Copyright © by The Psychoanalytic Quarterly

A C.I.P. for this book is available from the British Library

ISBN: 0 946439 61 3

www.karnacbooks.com

CONTENTS

INTRODUCTION

In the autumn of 1914 the demands of military service broke in upon the psychoanalytic activities of the author of this work and exiled him to a small garrison town, where he found the duties of chief medical officer to a squadron of Hussars somewhat of a contrast to the pressure of activity to which he had been accustomed. Thus he came to occupy his leisure hours with the translating of Freud's *Drei Abhandlungen zur Sexualtheorie;* and it was almost inevitable that he should have elaborated in his mind certain ideas suggested by this work and have set down, however sketchily, the results. These notions revolved around a fuller elucidation of the act of coitus, conceived in the *Abhandlungen* as the final phase in the total course of sexual development, to be sure, but not there dealt with in any detail from the standpoint of its evolution and development. These ideas gradually crystallized into an onto- and phylogenetic theory which in 1915 I submitted to Professor Freud on the occasion of a visit of his to my military station. Later, in 1919, I repeated the exposition of this theory before him and before a small group of friends, and on both occasions was urged to write it out for publication. My failure for some time to act upon this invitation, though due in part to resistances engendered by the singularity of my material, was determined also by objective considerations. My equipment in the natural sciences did not in any wise exceed that of a physician who in his time has studied various branches of natural science with every diligence and out of a special fondness for them, but who for nearly twenty years has not been concerned with them to any detailed extent. And yet my theory dealt with matters which were at that time the very center of biological discussion. I had at my disposal as works of reference only the fine Zoology of Hesse and Doflein, and one work each of Lamarck, Darwin, Haeckel, Bölsche, Lloyd Morgan, Godlewsky, H. Hertwig, Piéron and Trömner;

whereas the results of modern biological investigation, notably those concerned with the mechanics of development, were almost wholly unavailable to me.[1]

In my speculations on the problems of genitality I boldly transferred to animals, to their organs and the parts thereof, and to their tissues, all kinds of processes with which I had become acquainted through psychoanalysis; and if with the aid of this transposition I arrived at new points of view, I nevertheless became guilty of a psychomorphism which, as a methodological excess, weighed upon my scientific conscience. On the other hand, this train of thought compelled me to make use of observations on animals, data from embryology, etc., as aids in the explanation of mental states; as for example the status of the psyche during coitus, in sleep, and so forth. According to my conviction at that time this too was forbidden; indeed, I had learned in school to consider it a fundamental principle of scientific work to keep strictly separated from each other the respective points of view of the natural sciences and of the mental sciences. The fact that in my speculations this rule was more honored in the breach than the observance was one of the reasons which restrained me from publishing my theory of genitality.

However, at the time when I was immersed in the *Drei Abhandlungen,* I was extraordinarily impressed by the fact that Freud was able to evaluate experiences gained in the field of the treatment of the psychoneuroses, and therefore in the mental realm, in such a way as to be in a position to reconstruct with the aid of these an entire chapter of biology, namely, the knowledge of sexual development. And in the Foreword to my translation I extolled his work as a significantly forward step in scientific methodology, as the reestablishment of an animism no longer anthropomorphic.[2]

---

[1] For similar reasons I was compelled to limit my investigation of genital functioning to the vertebrates and could not take up the consideration of the extremely interesting case of the insects; nor was it possible to include the genital life of plants.

[2] This introduction has been published in the Int. Ztschr. f. Psa. III, (1915) under the title: *Die Wissenschaftliche Bedeutung von Freuds Drei Abhandlungen zur Sexualtheorie.*

Gradually the conviction grew upon me that such an importation into psychology of concepts belonging to the field of natural science, and into the natural sciences of psychological concepts, was inevitable and might be extremely fruitful. As long as one is satisfied with mere description, an exact tabulation of the details of a process is sufficient, and one is very easily able to confine oneself within one's own particular scientific boundaries. As soon, however, as one desires, in addition to description, to make some assertion regarding the *meaning* of a process, one involuntarily grasps for analogies in alien scientific fields. The physicist is able to make the phenomena of his science comprehensible only when he compares them to "forces", "attraction", "repulsion", to "resistance", "inertia", and the like—which are simply things with which we are acquainted from the mental side alone. But Freud also was compelled to reduce mental functioning to topographical, dynamic, economic, and therefore purely physical processes, for otherwise he was unable to approach their final explanation. Ultimately I perceived that we need not be ashamed of this reciprocal analogizing, that on the contrary it should be vigorously pushed as a highly necessary and, indeed, inevitable method. In later works I no longer had any hesitation, in fact, in recommending this working method, which I termed a "utraquistic" one; and I expressed the hope that it would enable science to answer even those questions in the face of which it had previously been helpless.

Once the right is granted to make freer use of analogies previously despised, it is perfectly obvious that these should be drawn from fields as remote as possible. Analogies derived from related fields would tend to be, indeed, mere tautologies, and as such could hardly serve the function of proof. In scientific statements which purport to be synthetic rather than analytic findings, the subject may not be repeated in the predicate; this is the familiar fundamental rule of every definition. Or, as a different approach, let us utilize the fact that materials are usually measured by a material of another kind; thus we easily may proceed to measure the material by the non-material, and *vice versa*.

The briefest formulation of this knowledge would be that all physical and physiological phenomena require a *meta*-physical (i.e., psychological) explanation and all psychological phenomena a meta-psychological (i.e., physical) one.

Emboldened by the acquisition of this insight and by the fact that the results at which I arrived with the aid of this method have found unexpected confirmation in the most recent and quite differently oriented investigations of others, I have decided upon the publication of the present volume.

Klobenstein am Ritten, August, 1923.

ONTOGENESIS

CHAPTER 1

AMPHIMIXIS OF EROTISMS IN THE EJACULATORY ACT

It was reserved for psychoanalysis to rescue the problems of sexuality from the poison cabinet of science in which they had been locked away for centuries. A certain perhaps necessitous sequence is clearly apparent, however, in the actual selection of the problems to which psychoanalysis has addressed itself. Just as in the matter of the sexual enlightenment of children even the most liberal approach boggles at the riddle of how the child comes to be in the mother's body, in the same way psychoanalysis has up to the present dealt to a relatively much greater degree with pregnancy and birth, with the acts preparatory to coitus, and with the perversions, than with the meaning and explanation of the phenomena of the act of coitus itself. I too must confess that the ideas which I should now like to communicate, at least in their broad outlines, have lain buried in my desk for more than nine years, and I suspect that my hesitancy in making them known—in giving birth to them, if you like—was attributable not alone to external causes but to my own resistances as well.

My reflections on the subject had their origin in certain psychoanalytic observations on impotence in the male. This seemed a promising lead; we know how often it is that what is in effect a caricature of normal functioning makes it possible to detect certain factors ordinarily masked and thus clarify the course of events in the normal process. Abraham, an especially zealous investigator of the so-called "pregenital organizations", has attributed *ejaculatio præcox* to a too intimate association of urethral erotism with genitality. Patients who suffer from premature ejaculation manifest the same attitude of indifference towards their semen as they would towards their urine, that is to say, as a valueless excretion of the organism. In contrast to this group of observations I have established the fact from a fairly

large number of cases that other patients are excessively economical of their semen, many of them so much so that they suffer, properly speaking, only from *impotentia ejaculandi;* that is,
they are capable of erection and intromission and are incapable
only of ejaculation.   In the unconscious and to some extent
even in the conscious mentation of these patients the equating
of coitus with the act of defæcation plays an important part
(equating of the vagina with the water-closet, of the semen with
fæces, etc.).   Not infrequently these patients have displaced
upon the sexual act the self-will and obstinacy with which in
childhood they opposed the strict regulation of their excretory
habits imposed on them by convention; they are impotent if
the partner desires intercourse, they have erections only when
the performance of the act is for some reason impossible or
impracticable (as for example in the case of menstruation), they
have outbreaks of rage or hatred or suddenly become cold if
their partner opposes their willfulness in the slightest imaginable degree.   It is easy, then, to assume in these patients as
intimate an association of anal elements with the acts of coitus
as Abraham has shown to be true of urethral elements in the
case of *ejaculatio præcox;* in other words, it has to be assumed
that there is such a thing as a specific *anal technique* in impotence in the male.

It then occurred to me that less pronounced disturbances of
the act of coitus similarly connected with anal functioning are
not especially uncommon.   Many men have a compulsion to
defæcate before performing the sexual act; moreover, severe
nervous digestive disorders may disappear when emotional
inhibitions of sexuality have been analytically resolved; one is
familiar too with the obstinate constipation which is a not
unusual consequence of excessive masturbation and squandering of semen.   Among the "character regressions" which I
have described I would cite as worthy of mention in this connection the case of men who, in other respects generous, are
very petty and even niggardly in the matter of giving money to
their wives.

To avoid misunderstanding I should remark that in the

psychoanalytic treatment of both anal and urethral impotence the psychic determinants of the disorder need not be sought in such a deep level of the biological substratum as in the case of the transference neuroses, in the œdipus complex and the related castration complex. The above-mentioned division of impotence into anal and urethral came about as a mere speculative by-product intended to indicate the ways in which the underlying motivation regressively enforces the overt appearance of the symptom. It should also be said that the two impotence mechanisms are almost never observed as separate entities; that much more often in actual practice a patient suffering from *ejaculatio præcox,* hence an urethral individual, acquires a capacity for erection and intromission in the course of the analysis but thereby loses temporarily his *potestas ejaculandi,* that is, he becomes aspermatic. In such patients it would seem that their original urethrality became converted into anality in the course of treatment. The result is an apparent super-potency, which however is satisfactory only to the patient's wife. It is only with the continuation or completion of the analysis that there is brought about a harmonizing, as it were, of the two opposed types of innervation and the establishing of satisfactory potency in consequence.

These observations have led me to suspect that in normal ejaculation a synergetic harmony of anal and urethral innervations is essential, their presence going unrecognized owing perhaps only to the fact that each innervation normally covers up or masks the other; whereas in *ejaculatio præcox* the urethral component, in *ejaculatio retardata* the anal, is alone in evidence.

The simple consideration of the nature of the sex act from the intromission of the penis to ejaculation would seem to support these assumptions. The terminal event of coitus, the ejaculation of semen, is undoubtedly an urethral phenomenon, which has in common with the voiding of urine not only its channel of excretion but the fact of being the ejection of a fluid under great pressure; on the other hand, during the frictional process inhibitory influences, in all probability of sphincteric origin, seem to assert themselves and to be capable, if they gain the upper hand to an untoward degree, of bringing about complete absence of ejaculation. Everything points to the fact that the urethral (i.e., ejaculatory) tendency is at work from the beginning, throughout the entire frictional process, and that in consequence an unceasing struggle occurs between the evacuatory and the inhibitory purpose, between expulsion and retention, in which the urethral element is eventually victorious. This two-fold innervation might, among other things, manifest itself also in the to-and-fro motion of the frictional process, in which penetration would correspond to the ejaculatory tendency, withdrawal to an ever recurring inhibition. Naturally one would have to ascribe significance also to the increase of excitement consequent upon continued friction, and to assume that this increase is capable, on exceeding a certain level, of finally overcoming the spasm of the sphincter.

This assumption presupposes a highly complicated and finely graduated coordination, a disturbance of which would produce just that ataxia and dyspraxia which one may describe as premature and inhibited emission. One is thereby forcibly reminded of a certain similarity between the anomalies of seminal emission of which I have spoken and the speech disorder which goes under the name of stuttering. In this instance, likewise, the normal flow of speech is assured by the proper coordination of the innervations necessary to the production of vowels and consonants. But if speech is interfered with from time to time by impeded vocalization or by the spasmodic character of the enunciation of consonants, there result the varieties of stuttering which specialists in speech disorders refer to as vocalic and consonantal stuttering. It is not difficult to guess that I should like to compare the innervation necessary to the production of tone with urethrality, and the interruptions of tone by consonantal sounds, which are in many ways suggestive of sphincter action, with anal inhibition. Yet that this is no mere superficial parallel but on the contrary has reference to a fundamental similarity between the two pathological conditions which goes much deeper, is attested by the remarkable fact that the disturbances of innervation which characterize stuttering are in fact traceable psychoanalytically to anal erotic sources on the one hand and to urethral erotic on the other. In a word, I should like to conceive the pathophysiological mechanism of disturbances of ejaculation as a kind of genital stuttering.

In this connection the embryological fact should not be disregarded that the penis, on which devolves the terminal act of coitus, the emission of semen, is *ab initio* adapted to the uniting of anal and urethral tendencies; for we must not forget that it grows out of the gut, or, in the lower mammals, out of the urogenital cloaca, as a quite late acquisition in developmental history.

Let us return from this physiological digression to our well-founded psychoanalytic knowledge and attempt to bring the situation as we have described it into line with Freud's sexual theory.

The sexual development of the individual culminates, according to the *Drei Abhandlungen,* in the supersession by the primacy of the genital zone of the hitherto active auto-erotisms (excitations of the so-called erotogenic zones) and of the previous organizations of sexuality, whereby the erotisms and the stages of organization which have been thus transcended are retained in the final genital organization as mechanisms of fore-pleasure. At this point, however, the question presents itself whether the analysis of the ejaculatory act into its separate elements, which we have attempted in the preceding paragraphs, does not supply a means of conjecturing, even if only partially, the subtler processes involved in the establishing of genital primacy. For what I described in physiological terms as a coordination of urethral and anal innervations may be expressed in the vocabulary of the sexual theory as a synthesis or an integration of anal and urethral erotisms into genital erotism. I may be permitted to emphasize this new conception by giving it a name of its own; let us term such a synthesis of two or more erotisms in a higher unity the *amphimixis* of erotisms or instinct-components.

But already this very first step towards a psychoanalytic theory of genitality encounters difficulties which seem to throw considerable doubt on its validity. One of these difficulties arises out of the fact that physiology fails to provide us with any means of conceiving how such an amphimixis might take place. Are actual nerve impulses transmitted from one organ to another or even from two organs to a third, or have we to do with chemical processes somewhat after the manner of an accumulation of endocrine products which reciprocally stimulate or inhibit one another? In all these matters we must confess our deep ignorance; but this particular difficulty should not by any means deter us from the pursuit of our theoretical considerations. For the explanation of a given process may be correct and from the standpoint of the psychoanalyst perfectly clear without the physiological side of the process being at the moment completely intelligible. Freud's entire sexual theory is a purely psychoanalytic one; the biological evidence for its correctness must be supplied subsequently by the physiologists.

A much more serious objection to the theory of amphimixis is a metapsychological one—more serious since it emanates from the field of psychoanalysis itself. Metapsychology has heretofore worked with the hypothesis of mechanisms which are charged with energy and from which energy is withdrawn. The difference in reactions was thought of as being caused by a difference in mechanism, whereas in the case of energy it was only the quantity and not the quality or character of it that mattered. We conceived of the mental always as a variety of mechanisms operated by one and the same energy, in such manner that this energy might shift from one system to another; but we have never spoken specifically of a shifting of qualities, above all of qualitative differences in the energies themselves, such as the amphimixis theory would demand. If we look more closely, however, we find that such a conception, even if only implicit, has underlain certain psychoanalytic views. I have in mind in particular the psychoanalytic conception of the phenomena of hysterical conversion and

materialization.[1] The latter we were obliged to consider as
a "heterotopic genital function", as a regressive genitalization
of earlier autoerotisms, or in other words as processes in which
typically genital erotisms, such as erectility, frictional activity,
and the ejaculatory tendency, constituting a qualitatively well-
defined syndrome, are displaced from the genital to innocuous
parts of the body. This "displacement from below upwards"
is very possibly nothing but a reversal of the amphimictic
downward trend of erotisms to the genital whereby, according
to the theory here propounded, the primacy of the genital
zone is established. Therefore, the metapsychological objection to the amphimixis theory need not disturb us any longer;
on the contrary, we ought to consider whether we shall not have
to exchange the conception of one energy but many mechanisms, attractive though this theory is by reason of its sim-
plicity, for that of a multiplicity of forms of energy. This we
have already unwittingly done, in that we have considered
psychic mechanisms as charged now with ego-tendencies, now
with sexual ones.

We are therefore not guilty of any inconsistency in working
with erotisms which are displaceable and capable of interopera-
tion, while preserving their qualitative individuality.

The question now presents itself whether the urethro-anal
amphimixis which I have described cannot be corroborated by
other kinds of linkages between these erotisms, whether other
characteristics of coitus can also be referred to similar mixtures
of erotisms, and finally whether these can be brought into
harmony with the sexual theory.

Between urethral and anal autoerotism there seems in fact
to exist a kind of reciprocity well prior to the establishing of
genital primacy. The child has a tendency to obtain an extra
dividend of pleasure from emptying the bladder and from
retaining the stool, but learns to renounce a part of this

[1] Ferenczi, S.: Hysterische Materialisationsphänomene, in: *Hysterie und
Pathoneurosen*, Int. Psa. Bibliothek, No. 2, Vienna, 1919. Trans. in *Further
Contributions to the Theory and Technique of Psycho-Analysis*, London, 1926.

pleasure in order to insure the love of those who take care of him.   But whence does the child derive the ability to follow the instructions of mother or nurse and overcome his prodigality with urine and his parsimony with fæces?   I believe that this ability is a result of the fact that the organs participating in urethral functioning are crucially influenced from the anal sphere, the organs of anal functioning from the urethral, so that the bladder acquires a degree of retentiveness from the rectum, the rectum a degree of liberality from the bladder—or, scientifically stated, by means of an amphimixis of the two erotisms in which the urethral erotism receives anal admixtures and the anal erotism urethral.   If this is so, we should have to ascribe to the constitution of the admixture and to the finer or grosser apportionment of the ingredients of this combination of erotisms, an enormous importance as regards not only genital normality or individuality but character formation in particular, which latter, as Freud has taught us, is to be regarded as in large measure the psychic superstructure and the psychic transcript of these erotisms.

Even apart from this consideration, the assumption of a urethro-anal amphimixis in the copulative act is notably facilitated by this pregenital amphimixis.   The genital would then no longer be the unique and incomparable magic wand which conjures erotisms from all the organs of the body; on the contrary, genital amphimixis would merely be one particular instance out of the many in which such fusion of erotisms takes place.   From the standpoint of individual adaptation this special instance is most significant, however; we see by what means in general the force of education brings about renunciation of pleasure and the adoption of an unpleasurable activity, namely, only by a clever combination of mechanisms of pleasure.   The bladder learns to retain urine only by making use of another type of pleasure, that of retention; and the bowel renounces the pleasure of constipation by borrowing from the urethral pleasure in voiding.   It is possible, perhaps, that in a sufficiently deep analysis the most successful sublimation, even an apparently complete renunciation, might be reduced to such hidden elements of hedonistic gratification, without which, apparently, no living organism can be induced to make any change in its activity.[1]

The question whether there occur other mixtures and trans-positions of erotisms can be answered categorically in the affirmative.[2]   Observation of children alone affords numerous indications of their existence.   Children are fond of fusing pleasurable activities of the most various kinds into a single act; they like in particular to combine the pleasure of eating with that of emptying the bowel; even infants, as Lindner, the first to make the observation, emphasized, are prone to combine thumb-sucking with rubbing or picking at various skin areas such as the lobe of the ear, the finger, or even the genital.   One may very properly speak of a mixture of oral and anal or of oral and skin erotisms in these instances.   Furthermore, the well-known activities of perverts customarily strive for such a sum-mation of erotisms, most conspicuously in those *voyeurs* who obtain gratification only by simultaneously watching the act of defæcation and smelling or eating fæces.   The most char-acteristic example of an amphimictically urethro-anal perform-ance I owe, however, to a two-year-old boy who would sit on a chamber and alternately pass a few drops of urine and a little fæces or flatus to the accompaniment of a continuous cry of, "*egy csurr, egy pú—egy csurr, egy pú*", which may be translated

---

[1] A similar mutual dependence on the part of the urethral spendthrift tendency and the anal inhibitory one is repeated, as I believe, in the struggle to give up masturbation.   The onanistic squandering of semen may rightly be regarded as a repetition of the enuretic period, while the hypochondriacal anxiety which impels the giving up of masturbation betrays unmistakable anal trends.

[2] Under certain circumstances bowel and bladder behave as though they had exchanged functions in a way which could be accounted for on the basis of an excessive influence of each of the two antagonistic innervations upon the other; for example, in nervous diarrhœa the bowel is inundated by urethrality: while in urinary retention of nervous origin the bladder overdoes the inhibition learned from the bowel.   In those cases in which I obtained an insight into the causes of such behavior, I found it to be a disguised expression of spite.   The child and the neurotic adult succeed in reducing educative measures to an absurdity by overdoing them.

into English, in the vernacular of childhood, as "now a pee, now a poop".

In a few patients I have even obtained some insight into the psychic motivation of such combinations; for example, an essentially anally impotent patient experienced a state of depression, fantasies of impoverishment and feelings of inferiority after every evacuation of the bowels, these being replaced during the consumption of the next meal by prodigious delusions of grandeur. This case demonstrates that the obvious combination of anal with oral erotism, namely, coprophagia, strives to atone for the pain of anal loss by the pleasure of oral incorporation.

As examples of the displacement of erotic qualities I may further mention the shifting of erotism from the clitoris to the vagina described by Freud, the shifting of the erectile tendency to the nipple and the nares, and the tendency to blushing (erection of the entire head) on the part of the maiden who represses sexual excitement.

The so-called synæsthesias, furthermore, in which the stimulation of a given sense organ is accompanied by the illusional stimulation of some other (audition colorée, vision acoustique, audition odorée, etc.), supply evidence for the existence of mixtures of erotic trends, according to the psychoanalytic observations which we owe to Pfister and to Hug-Hellmuth, among others.

All these observations which I have here set down in quite informal fashion have strengthened me in the preconceived notion that the act of ejaculation is a phenomenon of urethro-anal amphimixis. I would now venture to consider from this standpoint the dynamics of the act of coitus in its entirety, including its preparatory activities and those concerned with fore-pleasure.

CHAPTER 2

COITUS AS AN AMPHIMICTIC PHENOMENON

We know from the "sexual theory" that the activities characteristic of infantile erotism reappear in the adult sex act in the form of activities concerned with fore-pleasure, but that in the adult the actual discharge of the excitation only takes place at the moment of ejaculation. Whereas in the child, thumb-sucking, slapping and being slapped, looking and being looked at, are capable of yielding complete satisfaction, in the adult, looking, kissing, embracing, etc., serve only to set in motion the genital mechanism proper. Here, it is as though none of these latter excitations was carried through to a conclusion; it is, rather, as though they were transmuted into another erotism when the intensity of the excitation reached a certain degree. Excitement engendered by erotic looking, hearing and smelling, when it reaches a sufficient intensity, impels embracing and kissing, and it is only when these contacts have attained a certain vehemence that erection and the urge to intromission and friction result, to culminate in the amphimictic phenomenon of ejaculation above described. One might quite properly speak of a condensed recapitulation of sexual development as taking place in each individual sex act. It is as though the individual erotogenic zones were smouldering fires connected by a fuse which finally sets off the explosion of the charge of instinctual energy accumulated in the genital.

More probable, however, is the assumption that such an amphimictic displacement downwards takes place not alone during the sex act but throughout life; indeed this assumption has in its favor the heuristic argument that with its help we can form a more definite conception of the meaning and biological purpose of the achieving of genital primacy. The principal stages in the development of the libido are, as we know, those of the evolution from autoerotism *via* narcissism to genital object-love. In the autoerotic stage of this evolution the sexuality of each separate organ of the body or instinct-component exists in a state of anarchy which is lacking in all regard for the weal or woe of the rest of the organism. It necessarily signifies a definite advance with regard to the functional capacity—that is, the utility function—of the individual organs when it becomes possible continuously to turn aside sexual excitations from them and to store these up in a special reservoir from which they are periodically tapped. If there were no such separation of pleasure activities, the eye would be absorbed in erotic looking, the mouth would be exclusively utilized as an oral-erotic instrument, instead of being employed in necessary self-preservative activities; even the skin would not be the protective covering whose sensitiveness provides warning of danger, but would be merely the seat of erotic sensations; the musculature would not be the executive instrument of purposive volitional activity, but would subserve only the release of sadistic and other pleasurable motor discharges, etc. By ridding the organism of sexual cravings and concentrating these in the genital, the level of efficiency of the organism is definitely raised and its adaptation to difficult situations—to catastrophes, even—made possible. One must conceive of the genital center so to speak pangenetically, in Darwin's sense; that is to say, there is no part of the organism which is not represented in the genital, so that the genital, in the rôle of executive manager, as it were, provides for the discharge of sexual tension on behalf of the entire organism.

The development from autoerotism to narcissism would then be the even outwardly recognizable result of the amphimictic displacement downwards of all erotisms. If we wish to take seriously this provisional idea of the pangenesis of the genital function, then we may venture to regard the phallus as a miniature of the total ego, as the embodiment of a pleasure-ego, and to say that this duplication of the ego is for the narcissistic ego the fundamental prerequisite of love. For this miniature ego, which in dreams and other products of fantasy so often symbolically represents the total personality, conditions must be created in the sex act such as shall assure its gratification simply and certainly; and with these conditions we shall now, if only briefly, concern ourselves.

Psychoanalytic experience has established that the acts preparatory to coitus likewise have as their function the bringing about of an identification with the sexual partner through intimate contact and embraces. Kissing, stroking, biting, embracing serve to efface the boundaries between the egos of the sexual partners, so that during the sex act the man, for example, since he has as it were introjected the organ of the woman, need no longer have the feeling of having entrusted to a strange and therefore hazardous environment his most precious organ, the representative of his pleasure-ego; he can therefore quite easily permit himself the luxury of erection, since in consequence of the identification which has taken place the carefully guarded member certainly will not get lost, seeing that it remains with a being with whom the ego has identified itself. Thus there is brought about in the act of coitus a successful compromise between the desire to give out and the desire to retain, between an egoistic and a libidinal striving—a phenomenon which we have already met with in the double determination of all hysterical conversion symptoms. And indeed this analogy is no accidental one, since the hysterical symptom, as countless psychoanalytic observations have shown, is always a reproduction in some manner of genital functioning.

Once there has come about the most intimate possible union between two persons of opposite sex through ties created by kisses, embraces and the insertion of the penis, there then occurs the final and decisive battle between the desire to give away and the desire to keep the genital secretion itself, which at the beginning of our argument we ventured to describe as a struggle between anal and urethral strivings. In fine, therefore, the entire genital warfare rages about the issue of giving up or not giving up a secretory product the escape of which from the male body is permitted by the terminating ejaculation, thus freeing the man from sexual tension, but in a way which at the same time safeguards the security and welfare of this secretory product inside the body of the woman. This safeguarding, however, may clearly be assumed to constitute an identification between the sexual secretion and the ego, so that we should now have a threefold identification in connection with coitus: identification of the whole organism with the genital, identification with the partner; and identification with the sexual secretion.[1]

If now we survey the evolution of sexuality from the thumb-sucking of the infant through the self-love of genital onanism to the heterosexual act of coitus, and keep in mind the complicated identifications of the ego with the penis and with the sexual secretion, we arrive at the conclusion that the purpose of this whole evolution, therefore the purpose likewise of the sex act, can be none other than an attempt on the part of the ego—an attempt at the beginning clumsy and fumbling, then more consciously purposive, and finally in part successful—to return to the mother's womb, where there is no such painful disharmony between ego and environment as characterizes existence in the external world. The sex act achieves this transitory regression in a threefold manner: the whole organism attains this goal by purely hallucinatory means, somewhat as in sleep; the penis, with which the organism as a whole has identified itself, attains it partially or symbolically; while only the sexual secretion possesses the prerogative, as representative of the ego and its narcissistic double, the genital, of attaining *in reality* to the womb of the mother.

In the phraseology of the natural sciences we should have to say of the sex act that it purposes and attains a simultaneous gratification as regards both the soma and the germ-plasm. For the soma, ejaculation signifies being rid of a burdensome secretory product; for the sex cells entry into the *milieu* most favorable to them. The psychoanalytic conception teaches us,

---

[1] To meet an obvious objection, I would emphasize that this exposition deals exclusively with the simpler conditions pertaining to the male participant. I must postpone to a subsequent occasion the demonstration of the applicability of this conception to the more complicated conditions in the female sex.

however, that the soma (in consequence of its "identification" with the sexual secretion) not only gratifies by means of the ejaculation egoistic tendencies making for the release of tension, but, in the form of a hallucinatory and symbolic (partial) return to the womb so unwillingly left at birth, shares also in the real gratification of the germ cells—which latter we may call from the standpoint of the individual the libidinal side of the sex act.

In the light of this "bioanalytic" conception of genital processes, as I should like to term it, it becomes comprehensible for the first time why the œdipus wish, the wish for sexual intercourse with the mother, recurs so regularly, with an almost wearisome monotony, as the central striving in the analysis of the male. The œdipus wish is precisely the psychological expression of an extremely general biological tendency which lures the organism to a return to the state of rest enjoyed before birth.

One of the most gallant tasks of physiology would be the demonstration of those organic processes which make possible the summation of single erotisms into genital erotism. According to the hypothesis outlined above, whenever an organ fails to indulge its pleasure tendencies directly but renounces these in favor of the organism as a whole, substances may be secreted from this organ or qualitative or quantitative innervations be shifted to other organs and eventually to the genital, it being the task of the latter to equalize in the gratificatory act the free-floating pleasure tensions of all the organs.

For biology, however, there would arise the not less difficult problem of indicating the ways in which the striving for gratification on the part of the germ-plasm and the similar striving on the part of the individual soma, originally altogether independent of each other, achieve a fusion in the sex act or mutually influence each other. It would have to demonstrate the onto- and phylo-genetic causes which compel so many forms of life to seek their highest gratification precisely in the act of copulation, which according to the discussion here presented is nothing but the expression of the striving to return to the mother's womb.

CHAPTER 3

STAGES IN THE DEVELOPMENT OF THE EROTIC SENSE OF REALITY

In a previous work on the course of development of the reality sense in the growing child[1] I had already reached the conclusion that the human being is dominated from the moment of birth onwards by a continuous regressive trend toward the reestablishment of the intrauterine situation, and holds fast to this unswervingly by, as it were, magical-hallucinatory means, by the aid of positive and negative hallucinations. The full development of the reality sense is attained, according to this conception, only when this regression is renounced once and for all and a substitute found for it in the world of reality. This development is experienced, however, by only a part of the personality; in sleep and in dreams, in the sex life and the life of fantasy, the striving towards the fulfilment of that primordial wish is still clung to.

In what follows the attempt will be made to supplement to some extent this train of thought. We shall disclose the stages of the development of sexuality, described by Freud, as uncertain and fumbling yet increasingly outspoken attempts to attain the goal of returning to the maternal womb, whereas we must recognize in the final phase of the entire evolution—in the fully developed genital function, that is—the complete attainment of this goal. It was, indeed, indicated in the previous chapter that in the sex act one succeeds in a real sense, even if in only a partial one, in returning to the maternal womb. The fully developed genital function, therefore, may be called, by analogy with the reality sense, the attainment of the "erotic reality sense".

In the first oral erotic stage of infantile sexual organization those who take care of the child are still solicitous that the

---

[1] Ferenczi, S.: *Entwicklungsstufen des Wirklichkeitssinnes.* Int. Ztschr. f. Psa. I, 1913. (Trans. in *Contributions to Psychoanalysis.* Boston: Richard G. Badger, 1916.)

illusion of the intrauterine state is preserved to it; they provide the warmth, the darkness and the quiet which are requisite to that illusion.   The excretory functions are for the time being entirely uncontrolled, and the actual activity of the newborn infant is limited principally to sucking at the mother's breast. Indeed this first love-object is forced upon the child from the beginning by the mother, so that one may speak in the case of the child of a primary "passive object-love".   At all events the rhythmicity of sucking remains permanently fixed as an essential ingredient of every subsequent erotic activity, and becomes incorporated—as we believe, amphimictically—in the act of masturbation and coitus.   The purely libidinal activity of this period, thumb-sucking or *Wonnesaugen* (Lindner), is also the first problem of erotism that we encounter.   What is it that impels the infant to continue sucking even after the appeasal of his hunger; what is it in this activity that affords him pleasure?   We will postpone an attempt to solve this riddle and along with it the fundamental problem of the psychology of erotism until we have considered other erotisms in detail.

The nursling is in the main an ectoparasite on its mother, just as in the fœtal period it lived on her endoparasitically. And just as it lorded it in the mother's womb and finally compelled the mother, its liberal host, to put the presumptuous guest out of doors, so also it behaves more and more aggressively towards the nursing mother.   It emerges from the period of harmless oral erotism, sucking, into a cannibalistic stage; it develops within the mouth implements for biting with which it would fain eat up, as it were, the beloved mother, compelling her eventually to wean it.   Now what we mean by this is not only that this cannibalistic trend subserves the instinct of self-preservation; we suppose, rather, that the teeth are employed also as weapons in the service of a libidinal striving; they are implements with the help of which the child would like to bore its way into its mother's womb.

The sole argument—at all events the argument of moment to the psychoanalyst—which emboldens us to offer this daring hypothesis is the uniformity and unmistakableness with which the symbolic identity of penis and tooth recurs, both in dreams and in neurotic symptoms. According to our conception the tooth is therefore really a primal penis *(Urpenis)*, whose libidinal rôle, however, the child who has been weaned must learn to renounce.[1] It is not that the tooth is therefore the symbol of the penis but rather, to speak paradoxically, that the later maturing penis is the symbol of the more primitive boring implement, the tooth. The paradoxical character of this supposition is perhaps moderated, however, by the consideration that every symbolic association is preceded by a stage in which two things are treated as one and so can represent each other.

Cannibalism, indeed, contains in part those aggressive elements which manifest themselves so obviously in the ensuing sadistic-anal organization. The so strikingly intimate connection between anal libido and expressions of sadism would be, in the sense of the foregoing argument, a displacement of originally "cannibalistic" aggressiveness upon intestinal function. The motive for this displacement is the reaction of displeasure called forth in the child by the necessity for observing certain toilet regulations set by parent or nurse. Furthermore, the oral-erotic regression to the mother which was earlier attempted is not given up in this period; it now returns as identification of the stool with a child, that is, with the subject's own self. It is as though the child produced a kind of introversion of his libido after the rather demoralizing parrying of his oral-erotic aggression on the part of the mother; by being womb and child (fæces) in his own person, he makes himself independent of the nurse (mother) in a libidinal sense. This is perhaps the fundamental basis of that character trait of stubbornness into which the anal-sadistic libido is usually converted.

The period of masturbation is to be considered as the first stage of the beginning primacy of the genital zone and thus as

---

[1] A two-year-old child said on seeing his newborn brother at the breast, "Danny eats meat". The strict Jewish injunction against eating meat and milk simultaneously is perhaps only an arrangement for insuring weaning.

a special stage of development of the libido.[1] Our analyses show unequivocally that large quantities of anal and sadistic libido are associated with masturbatory activity, so that we are now able to trace the displacement of the aggressive components from the oral phase *via* the anal to the genital. In masturbation, however, the symbolic equation: child=fæces, is superseded by that of child=penis, so that in the male child the hollow of his own hand plays the part of the maternal genital. We notice that in the last two phases the child usually plays a double rôle which is certainly related to the fact of infantile bisexuality. At all events it is extraordinarily important for the understanding of the manifestations of the fully developed genital libido, that every human being, whether male or female, can and does enact with his own body the double rôle of the child and of the mother.

In the last phase of development of the infantile libido the child returns, after the periods of passive object-love, after cannibalistic aggression and introversion, to the original object, the mother, but this time equipped with a more suitable weapon of attack. The erectile penis finds of itself the way to the maternal vagina, and would attain this goal did not the taboos of convention or perhaps a special defense mechanism or anxiety bring about a speedy end to this precocious œdipus love.

We will forego the description of the sexual periods now following, the period of latency and that of puberty, since the task which we set ourselves was only that of proving that the ontogenesis of sexuality unswervingly adheres to the striving to return to the womb, and that the genital organization, which is the vehicle of this striving, represents a culminating point in the development of the erotic reality sense. After the first unsuccessful oral attempt to regain the mother's womb, there follow the so to speak *autoplastic* periods of anality and of masturbation in which a fantasied substitute for the lost love-

[1] Very recently Freud has described a special "phallic" stage of organization—Int. Ztschr. f. Psa. IX, 1923. (Freud: *The Infantile Genital Organization of the Libido: A Supplement to the Theory of Sex.* Coll. Papers II, 244–250.)

object is sought for in the subject's own body; but only through the instrumentality of the male organ of copulation is the first serious attempt made to realize, this time *alloplastically,* the striving to return to the womb, first on the mother herself, then on all the other female persons in the environment.

We can fulfil only sketchily the task of representing the genital process as ultimately achieved, as the amphimictic summation of earlier erotisms. Aggressive impulses are manifested in the sex act in the violence of possession of the sexual object and in penetration itself. Upon the utilization of anal and oral erotism in the construction of the *parental erotism* so intimately connected with genitality we shall attempt to throw a little light in the discussion now to follow, which may no longer be postponed, of the modes of development of female sexuality.

The development of genital sexuality, cursorily described above in the male, undergoes in the female a rather sudden interruption. It is characterized above all else by the displacement of erogeneity from the clitoris (the female penis) to the cavity of the vagina. Psychoanalytic experience compels the assumption, however, that not alone the vagina but, in the manner of hysteria, other parts of the body as well are genitalized, in particular the nipple and the surrounding area. It is probable that in nursing something of the lost pleasure of intromission and ejaculation gains satisfaction, and indeed the nipple exhibits definite erectility. But apparently considerable amounts of oral and anal erotism are displaced also upon the vagina, the unstriated musculature of which seems to imitate in its spasmodic contractions as in its peristalsis the oral pleasure of ingestion and the anal of retention. For the leading zone of genitality, in which in the male the emphasis is definitely upon the urethral, regresses again in the female chiefly to the anal, in that in the sex act the accent is shifted to sheltering the penis and its secretion and also the fruit thereof *(parental erotism).* But in addition the partly abandoned male striving to return to the maternal womb is not altogether given up, at any rate in the psychic sphere, where it expresses itself as a fantasied identification, in coitus, with the penis-possessing male, and as the vaginal sensation of possessing a penis ("hollow penis"), as well as an identification on the part of the woman with the child that she harbors within her own body. Masculine aggressiveness turns into a passive pleasure in experiencing the sex act (masochism), which is explicable in part on the ground of very archaic instinctual forces (the death instinct of Freud), in part on that of the mechanism of identification with the conquering male. All these secondary recathexes of spatially remote and genetically superseded pleasure mechanisms in the female sex seem to have been instituted more or less by way of consolation for the loss of the penis.

Of the transition on the part of the woman from (masculine) activity to passivity one may form the following general idea: the genitality of the female penis is absorbed regressively into the whole body and into the whole ego of the woman, out of which—amphimictically, as we believe—it had arisen, so that a secondary narcissism becomes her portion; on the erotic side, therefore, she becomes again more like a child who wants to be loved, and is thus a being who still clings *in toto* to the fiction of existence in the mother's womb. In this way she can then easily identify herself with the child in her own body (or with the penis as its symbol) and make the transition from the transitive to the intransitive, from active penetration to passivity. The secondary genitalization of the female body also explains her greater proneness to conversion hysteria.[1]

To observe the genital development of the female is to obtain the impression that on the occasion of the first sexual intercourse this development is still quite uncompleted. The first attempts at coitus are so to speak only acts of rape in which even blood must flow. It is only later that the woman learns to experience the sex act passively, and later still to feel it as pleasurable or even to take an active part in it. Indeed, in the individual sex act the initial defense is repeated in the form

---

[1] Ferenczi, S.: "Hysterische Materialisationsphänomene"; in *Hysterie und Pathoneurosen*, Int. Psa. Bibliothek, No. 2, Vienna, 1919. (Trans. in *Further Contributions to the Theory and Technique of Psycho-Analysis*, London, 1926.

of a muscular resistance on the part of the narrowed vagina; it is only later that the vagina becomes lubricated and easy of entrance, and only later still that there occur the contractions which seem to have as their purpose the aspiration of the semen and the incorporation of the penis—the latter certainly an intended castration as well. These observations, together with certain phylogenetic considerations which will occupy us more fully later, suggested to me the conception that one phase of the warfare between the sexes is here repeated individually—a phase in which the woman comes off second best, since she cedes to the man the privilege of penetrating the mother's body in a real sense, while she herself contents herself with fantasy-like substitutes and particularly with harboring the child whose fortune she shares.[1] At all events, according to the psychoanalytic observations of Groddeck, there is vouchsafed to the female, even in childbirth and hidden behind the painfulness of labor, a meed of pleasure which is denied to the male sex.

In the light of these considerations the modes of gratification of perverts and the symptoms of psychoneurotics receive a new illumination. The fixation of such individuals at a lower stage of sexual development would thus be only an incomplete attainment of the ultimate goal of the erotic reality function, the genital reestablishment of the intrauterine situation. And even neurasthenia, the archetype of the "actual neurosis", which is associated with *ejaculatio præcox*, and anxiety neurosis, which is characterized by a tendency to excessive retention, can now be explained on the ground of an excessive addition to genitality of elements in part urethral, in part anal, and the resulting impotence be traced analytically to anxiety concerning the intrauterine situation.

I doubt not that this train of thought will find striking confirmation in the observation of the sexual life of animals, and I regret only that I lack access to this field of knowledge. The slight acquaintance with it that I possess seems to support my

---

[1] This is in brief the construction I attempted to which Freud refers in his paper on *The Taboo of Virginity* (Coll. Papers IV, 217–236).

conception of the universality of the trend of maternal regression and its undoubted prominence in the sex act. I refer, for example, to the fact that in many animals the sex act is of well-nigh interminable duration.[1]

[1] In spiders coitus may last for seven hours, and in the frog for four weeks. It has long been known that a permanent union of the sexes occurs in many parasites, such that, for example, the male remains throughout life in the gullet or the uterus of the female. A peak of erotic reality development is attained, one might say, by those parasites that transfer almost the entire responsibility for their sustenance to the host and whose organization subserves predominantly the sex function.

CHAPTER 4

INTERPRETATION OF THE INDIVIDUAL PHENOMENA IN THE SEX ACT

After the foregoing considerations it will be worth while to subject to analysis, as though they were neurotic symptoms, the separate processes involved in the sex act. Of these we have so far devoted particular attention only to ejaculation.

There is above all the phenomenon of erection, for which a seemingly surprising explanation deriving from the maternal womb theory of genitality presents itself. I assume that the permanent invagination of the glans penis within a fold of mucous membrane (within the foreskin, that is) is itself nothing but a replica in miniature of existence in the maternal womb. Since upon an increase of the sexual tension accumulated in the genital the most sensitive portion of the penis (which, as already said, functions as the narcissistic representative of the total personality) is thrust out of its protected place of repose by erection, is, as it were, born, the sensation of unpleasure (*Unlust*) in the genital is suddenly distinctly increased; and this latter fact makes intelligible the sudden urge to restore the lost *milieu* by intromission into the vagina, or in other words, to seek in the external world of reality, this time actually within a female body, the hitherto autoerotically satisfying place of repose.

But in the sex act in man frictional movements of some duration precede ejaculation, for the understanding of which a rather lengthy exposition will be necessary.

In certain animals, so the zoologists tell us, there occurs the peculiar reaction known as *autotomy*, consisting in the fact that organs which irritate or otherwise annoy the animal are simply detached from the rest of the body by the action of certain muscles, or, in the literal sense of the word, dropped. There are, for example, worms which are able under such circumstances to extrude the entire intestine from the body; others break into small pieces. The ease with which the lizard leaves its tail behind in the grasp of its pursuer, only to have it quickly regenerate, is a matter of common knowledge. I do not hesitate to see in this type of reaction a fundamental property of all life and to assume that it represents a biological antecedent stage of repression, of withdrawal of cathexis from the painful.

Now we said at the beginning that all the kinds and amounts of unpleasure (*Unlust*) which, sidetracked during the period of utility functioning of all the organs, were left undealt with, undisposed of, are accumulated in the genital and thence discharged. This discharge can be nothing else than the desire, in the sense of an autotomy, to cast off the organ under tension. From the standpoint of the ego we have already described ejaculation as such an elimination of material productive of "unpleasure"; we may assume a similar tendency also in the case of erection and friction. Further, erection is perhaps only an incompletely achieved attempt to detach the genital, charged with "unpleasure" of various kinds, from the rest of the body. As in the case of ejaculation we may assume here also a struggle between tendencies in the direction of desiring to detach and desiring to retain, but which does not in this case end in the victory of the former.[1] Or one could suppose that the sex act begins as a tendency in the direction of the complete detaching of the genital and thus as a kind of self-castration, but is then satisfied with the detachment of its secretion. The manifold character of sexual behavior in animals permits observation in extreme examples of the varying outcome of this struggle. The armadillo *Dasypus* inserts in the female organ a penis which is enormous in proportion to the size of its body; the penis of the giraffe, on the contrary, gradually tapers on penetration in the manner of a telescope, to end in a filiform appendage through which the ejaculate is conveyed directly into the uterus.

The impulse to genital friction suggests the conjecture that the unpleasure accumulated in the whole body is stored in the

---

[1] In the autotomic tendency may also be found the final basis of the tooth-extraction symbolization of loss of semen and of birth.

genital in the form of an itching, which is then removed by a
kind of scratching. Now the scratching reflex is itself, we
presume, only an archaic vestigium of the autotomy tendency,
that is, an attempt to tear away the itching part of the body
with the nails; actual relief of the itching comes about in reality
for the most part only on scratching the itching area to the
point of bleeding and thus by means of an actual tearing away
of portions of tissue. It is conceivable that erection, friction
and ejaculation constitute, then, a process of autotomy, violent
at the outset, later moderated, which begins with the intention
of casting off the entire organ, then becomes limited to scratching (frictional movements), to be satisfied eventually with the
elimination of a fluid. It is self-evident, however, that this
characterizes only one aspect of the process—the ego or soma
aspect; from the standpoint of the germ-plasm, or of the libido,
this same process is a striving, manifesting itself with dimin-
ished vehemence, to return to the maternal womb.

To the deeper motives of the genital self-castration tendency
we will return later. It need only be noted here that there
exist countless examples of actual self-castration in the animal
kingdom, such that not merely is a secretion eliminated in the
sex act but the penis is even torn off. One may also refer in
this connection to the *annulus tendinosus* on the penis of the
Canidæ which causes the "hanging" of the male in the female
genital and suggests to the observer the idea of the possibility
of the penis being broken off.

The active courtship which precedes actual mating has
become attenuated in man in the course of the development of
civilization, often to the point of being quite unrecognizable,
in such a way that again we can recognize its meaning only
through the observation of animals. We have already mentioned that according to our assumption the central striving to
return to the maternal womb dominates both sexes equally;
courting can accordingly have as its purpose nothing else than
that the female sex, in giving up or in restricting her own real
gratification, be made amenable to tolerating the sex act on
the part of the male. We should like to cite in support of this

assertion two pronouncements of Charles Darwin, who can surely speak with authority on the question. "As appearances more than once lead us to believe", he says somewhere, "the female does not take the male that seems most attractive to her but the one that is least repulsive to her." In this conception is also expressed the preferential position of the male sex in the sex act which we have emphasized. In another place Darwin states that sexual variation in the sense of a sexual dimorphism always originates in the male sex, even if it is later adopted in part by the female also. All this agrees strikingly with Freud's assertion that all libido is *per se* "masculine", even when, as in the female, it seeks goals of gratification of a passive type.

We are of the opinion that the secondary sexual characters which thus originally belong only to the male are employed as weapons in a struggle in which it is a question of which combatant can achieve by force the sexual penetration of the body of the partner as substitute for the maternal womb. If we examine into the *modus operandi* of these weapons, we find that they all of them have every appearance of making the female amenable by sheer force or of paralyzing her by fascinating her hypnotically. In the former category belong for example the callosities on the thumb which develop in the male frog at the mating season and which penetrate into the axillæ of the female; in this sense also the greater body size of the male as compared with the female operates, and similarly the procedure of the males among certain reptiles which by beating a tattoo on the head of the female with their forelimbs render her submissive. Still more frequently subjugation of the female is accomplished by frightening her, by inflating the body or some part of it (as in the toad and the chamæleon), by expanding a large lobe of skin, a fleshy appendage, a goitre (as in many birds), or by the sudden great lengthening and elevation of the nose (observation by Darwin on sea-elephants). In one species of seal *(Cristophora cristata)* the male develops at the time of mating a folding cap which is larger than the head. The intimidation of the female by roars and outcries, which is of common occurrence, is perfectly familiar (cats, for example). To the same effect is the behavior of the male of a species of Malayan lizard which approaches the female in the mating season with the forward part of the body upraised in such a way that on the greatly distended laryngeal pouch every dark spot stands out in strong relief against a yellowish-red background. This manner of courtship seems, however, to contain, in addition to intimidation, elements of fascination through the sense of beauty, and is manifested in much more definite fashion in the display of magnificence of color, in the action of sound-producing mechanisms, in the production of light (in the fern beetle), and in the mating rituals, dancing, spreading the tail, flights of song and the decoy song of so many birds.

The first analogy which forces itself upon one in the consideration of these phenomena is, as already mentioned, that with hypnosis. On the basis of psychoanalytic observations we have been obliged to distinguish two means of inducing a state of hypnotic submission. We have called these father- and mother-hypnosis.[1] The former paralyzes its victim by intimidation, the latter through ingratiation. In both cases, in our opinion, the hypnotized person regresses to the level of an intimidated child; the peculiar cataleptic attitudes of the hypnotized render it easy to assume, however, that a deep regression to the maternal womb is also involved (Bjerre). In view of the general bisexuality of beings that reproduce sexually we shall no longer be astonished by the fact that as regards secondary sexual characters and their activity the male so frequently takes over the characteristic of beauty which I have emphasized as feminine and the feminine function of lulling to sleep. We conjecture therefore that in the course of courtship the female is duped by a hypnotic regression to the maternal womb, and that this fantastic situation of happiness indemnifies her for the endurance of the intrinsically non-pleasurable sex act. If, however, as the zoologists do, we consider all bodily

[1] Ferenczi, S.: *Introjektion und Übertragung.* Jahrb. f. Psa. I, 1909. (Trans.: Introjection and Transference, in *Contributions to Psychoanalysis,* 1916.)

sexual apparatus which is not directly concerned with the elaboration of sex secretion as belonging in the category of secondary sexual characters, then we must also properly consider as such the organs of copulation, the penis and vagina. And in fact one cannot escape the impression that the ostentation in regard to the sexual organs, the display of the penis, the exhibition of the vagina, exerts in itself an influence of fascination, that is to say, is capable of arousing the fantasy of the intrauterine situation in the partner who looks on.

Among the means of allurement those which make use of odors of a particular kind deserve special emphasis. The rôle of the odor of valerian in rutting cats is well known, as is also that of goats and of musk, and the power of attraction of the female butterfly, which has been observed to attract males to the city from a meadow many miles distant. It admits of no doubt, at any rate, that the special odor of the female genital has a sexually exciting effect also in the higher animals and in man, even if only through the fact that this odor awakens the longing for the mother's womb. The rabbit, for example, becomes impotent if his olfactory nerves are cut. We must not overlook the fact that the very first and foremost sense impressions of the child—fraught with significance, accordingly, for the whole of life—occur during birth and therefore in the birth canal (Groddeck).

The general attitude of the participants during the sex act itself, the emotions which they manifest during it, have received the least consideration up to the present. As if with regard to these affects the human being would guard his deepest secrets, a well-nigh insuperable feeling of shame prevents him from giving information about them. Even in analysis, where the analysand has to communicate all his reactions, he learns only at long last and only if necessary to describe his subjective train of experiences in the sex act, long after he has become accustomed to stating its objective events without reservation. What I have on occasion been able to gather amounts to this: The individual is dominated from beginning to end by a compulsive attraction to the sexual partner; he feels himself compelled by every means possible to do away with the separation in space between himself and the partner (see Chapter II, paragraph 5, on the tendency of *Brückenbildung:* kissing, embracing). One is forced to maintain that the mutual attraction is nothing but the expression of the fantasy of veritably merging one's self with the body of the partner or perhaps of forcing one's way *in toto* into it (as a substitute for the mother's womb); the ultimate sexual union is only the partial realization of this purpose. The tension which during coitus keeps the participants in a kind of suspense is in itself unpleasurable, and only the expectation of its prospective relief makes it at the same time pleasurable. This kind of unpleasurable tension has a good deal of similarity to anxiety, which, as we know from Freud, is always a reproduction of the unpleasurable sensations connected with the shock attending the process of being born.

It seems that we must accustom ourselves to the idea of the overdetermination of one and the same phenomenon in explaining physiological processes also, as psychoanalysis has taught us is true of psychological processes. The more closely we observe the phenomena of the sex act, the more evident it becomes that the latter is not only a pleasurably toned process (that is, the representation of the happy intrauterine situation) but that it also reproduces painful occurrences (probably the first emotion of anxiety in connection with birth). It is still more probable that these affects are not manifested in haphazard fashion but in an historically predetermined sequence. The increase of painful tension and its culmination in orgasm would thus be the simultaneous representation of two opposite tendencies: the repetition of the unpleasurable birth situation with its happy issue in the accomplishing of birth, and the reestablishing of the still quite undisturbed intrauterine situation by reentering the maternal womb.

The most striking physical concomitants of these emotions are manifested in the respiration and the circulation of the participants in the sex act. The respiration is obviously dyspnœic, the pulse rate increased; it is only with orgasm that a full and satisfying expiration and a subsiding of the heart rate occur. These disturbances suggest a recapitulation of the process of accomplishing that extensive adjustment which the change from the fœtal to the extrauterine mode of oxygen supply demands. Whether in drawing an analogy between coitus and the birth process one can go so far as to conceive of the rhythmicity of coitus as an abbreviated repetition of the rhythmicity of labor pains I should like to leave undecided.[1]

We must not omit to mention that coitus is accompanied by decidedly aggressive affects as well. This component, which was traced as far as the stage of genitality in Chapter 3, manifests itself during the sex act in increasingly violent muscular movements which not only have the holding fast of the love-object as their purpose but also betray unequivocally sadistic trends (biting, scratching). Even the earliest manifestations of life on the part of the newborn infant point to the fact that the trauma experienced during birth, especially the imprisonment in the birth canal, evokes not only anxiety but rage as well, which latter has equally to attain repetition in the act of coitus.[2]

The condition of the participants in the sex act during and after orgasm is characterized above all by an extensive reduction or even complete cessation of consciousness, which until then had been confined to and concentrated upon the striving to attain the genital goal. Examples from the animal kingdom certainly exhibit for us still more clearly this concentrating upon the feeling of gratification, which here amounts to a complete abolition also of sensitiveness to pain. There are species of lizards which let themselves be torn in pieces but do not interrupt the sex act, batrachians which are not disturbed in the sex act by mutilation. The rabbit lapses into a kind of catalepsy with orgasm, dropping unconscious and remaining

[1] The close relationship between anxiety and libido is one of the foundations of Freud's teaching. Even Freud's earliest publications made reference to the similarity between the symptoms of anxiety neurosis and the emotions characterizing coitus.

[2] Possibly the feeling of impotent rage is an important integral part of the affect of anxiety.

for some time motionless beside the female with the penis in the vagina. It would be only consistent to interpret these states and the feeling of complete satisfaction and absence of desire accompanying them, as the unconscious hallucinatory attainment of the goal of coitus on the part of the individual as a whole, the attainment of the intrauterine state, with the simultaneous symbolic and real attainment of this goal by the genitalia and the sex cells. Probably, however, the happy overcoming of the trauma of birth is herein represented as well. We shall presently have more to say about the changes of cathexis which presumably take place in connection with orgasm, and will content ourselves for the present with the foregoing description.

In conclusion I should like only to refer to the fact that both in the human being and among many species of animals, an intimate relationship exists between the procreative function and sleep. Certainly this corresponds to our theoretical expectation, since we consider both sleep and the sex act as regressions to the intrauterine situation. With the analogies and the differences between the two we shall be more fully concerned later on, but at this point we should like to remark that many animals, including the human species, readily fall asleep after coitus. According to psychoanalytic experience the majority of cases of insomnia of psychogenic origin are traceable to disturbances of sexual functioning and are curable only through their removal.

CHAPTER 5
GENITAL FUNCTIONING IN THE INDIVIDUAL

We may now ask ourselves whether on the basis of these and similar observations on the course and ontogenetic development of the procreative function we are finally in a position to predicate anything with regard to the meaning of this phenomenon which recurs periodically with such remarkable uniformity in so large a proportion of the animal kingdom.

Considered from a purely physiological standpoint, coitus seemed to us to be the periodically occurring terminal episode in the equalizing and adjustment of an unpleasure-producing state of libidinal tension which accumulates throughout the entire life of the individual as an accompaniment of every non-erotic activity on the part of the various organs and which is transferred from these organs to the genital in an "amphimictic" manner. In the processes which make up the procreative function are therefore brought together the total amounts and kinds of unsatisfied libido of all organs, and in particular of all erotogenic zones and stages of organization which have been abandoned in adulthood. Without being able to give more than an intimation of the nature of the physiological processes which play their part therein, we refer to the analogy between the terminal event in the act of coitus and the functions of excretion, and conjecture that in the phenomena of erection and ejaculation (which, as we know, are also adumbrated in the female) all those autotomic tendencies are summated, the carrying out of which was neglected by "utility functioning". A being with a developed genital function is therefore better adapted with reference also to the nonerotic activities concerned with the demands of existence; he can defer erotic gratification until the latter no longer interferes with the functions of self-preservation. One may therefore maintain that the genital also is an organ of "utility" which promotes the ends of the reality function.

We can form only an extremely unclear idea with regard to the changes in cathexis which take place after sexual gratification, and only with regard to the psychological aspect of orgasm would we make bold to express a somewhat more concrete point of view.   It looks as if under the conditions of coitus a tension which has been keyed up to a maximum is released unexpectedly and extremely easily, so that a large amount of cathectic energy becomes suddenly superfluous.   Hence the enormously great sensation of pleasure which here too, as in the case of the pleasure in wit, according to Freud, might be attributable to an economizing of cathectic energy.[1]   To this sensation some "genitofugal" backflow of libido into the bodily organs might run parallel, the opposite of that "genitopetal" flow which conducted the excitation from the organs to the genital during the period of tension.   At the moment of this backflowing of libido from the genital to all the rest of the psychophysical organism there occurs that ineffable feeling of bliss in which the utility function of the organs finds its reward and at the same time its inducement to renewed activity.[2]

The process in genital gratification consists so to speak in an eruptive genitalization of the entire organism, the complete identification, attained with the help of the frictional process, of the entire organism with the executive organ.

Be this manner of regarding the procreative process from the standpoint of the psychophysical economy ever so attractive, it throws no light on the question of why the accumulation and discharge of sexual energy have assumed just this form in so large a proportion of the animal kingdom; without an answer to this question we cannot have a feeling of its adequate determination.   We have learned from psychoanalysis that such a lack, at least in regard to psychic processes, can be remedied if

[1] To a similar economy of expenditure is also to be attributed the sensuous feeling of tickling.   Moreover, the majority of "ticklish" parts of the body may be genitalized, especially the axilla.

[2] The idea of the genitopetal stream of libido and its reverse course in orgasm was touched upon by the author as early as 1912 at the symposium held in Vienna on onanism (Über Onanie).

the purely ontological (descriptive-economic) point of view be supplemented by the historical and genetic. Accordingly we attempted to derive the instinctual manifestations of sexuality, as previously the manifestations of the reality sense, from the striving to reëstablish the antenatal situation, as a compromise between this striving, which seems to be completely renounced in actual life but in fact is only thrust to one side, and the obstacles which reality places in its way. The stages of sexual development described by Freud therefore appear to us as a continually repeated attempt to reattain that goal—the genital organization itself, however, as a final even if only partial attainment of that which is demanded by the instinct. Now it seems, on the other hand, that this instinctual gratification cannot achieve its goal directly, but must always repeat the genetic history of the instinct itself; in other words, it must repeat the adaptive struggle, itself unpleasant, which the individual must pass through in connection with the disturbing of an earlier pleasurable situation. The first and severest adaptive struggle in the life of every single creature was the harassing experience of birth and the task of adaptation which the change of environment enforced. We indeed supposed that coitus not only signifies the partly fantasied and partly real return to the maternal womb but contrives to represent in its symptomatology both birth anxiety and its overcoming in successful birth. But it is ingeniously arranged in coitus that the amount of anxiety shall not exceed a certain level, and even more ample provision is furnished that this anxiety shall be converted by the sudden almost complete attainment of the goal of gratification (the body of the woman) into enormous pleasure.

We can bring this hypothesis into connection with the examples which Freud adduced by way of illustrating the repetition compulsion in Beyond the Pleasure Principle (1921). The value of this comparison will perhaps be enhanced by the fact that it arrives at the results in question on the basis of quite different assumptions.

Certain symptoms of traumatic neurosis and certain remarkable peculiarities of children's play are explained by Freud on the basis of a compulsion to discharge in a gradual manner by means of countless repetitions, but always in small fractions only, undischarged excitations which on account of their intensity may not be discharged *en bloc*. We too consider coitus as such a partial discharge of that still unassimilated shock which is the legacy of the birth trauma; at the same time it appears to be like a game, or, more exactly expressed, a commemoration celebrating a happy liberation from bondage; finally it represents the hallucinatory denial of the trauma altogether.

We can give no consistent answer, at least as regards the procreative instinct, to the question raised by Freud as to whether the repetition is a compulsion or a desire, whether it lies this side of or beyond the pleasure principle. We believe that in so far as it gradually adjusts the traumatic effect just referred to it is a compulsion, that is, a reaction of adaptation compelled by an external disturbance. In so far, however, as the actual disturbance is therein denied in a negative hallucinatory manner or the memory of its overcoming celebrated, we have to do with pure pleasure mechanisms.

There is much that points to the fact that instinctual energies are unequally apportioned between soma and germ-plasm; it is as though the greater part of the instincts which are undisposed of were stored up in the germ-plasm, and as though therefore there emanated from the latter in special measure the traumatic repetition compulsion which discharged a part of the unpleasure *(Unlust)* with each repetition, each coitus. One is tempted to ascribe the self-castration tendencies which are manifested in the sex act to the striving to extrude from the body wholly or in part the sexual matter so productive of unpleasure. Simultaneously, however, the gratification of the individual soma on its own account is also taken care of in coitus, that is, in the form of a delayed dealing with the petty traumata of life, which are thus settled in a way tantamount to play.

In this playfulness we see the purely pleasurable element in genital gratification, and we believe that with its aid we are finally in a position to say something general about the psychology of erotism.

The majority of instinctual activities are set in motion, as we know, in connection with disturbances which impinge upon the organism from without or in connection with equally distressful changes in the interior of the body.   In the case of the play instincts, however, among which the erotic may in a certain sense also be reckoned, the instinct itself creates a state of unpleasure *(Unlust)* in order to enjoy the pleasure of doing away with it.   The playful and the erotic are therefore characterized by the fact that, in contrast to the usual situation in which the condition of tension occurs unexpectedly, the unpleasure is in the first place permitted only in known and measured dosage, and in the second place the possibility of removing or doing away with it is provided from the beginning, often indeed to a superabundant degree.   From this standpoint I should like to consider hunger, for example, in the light of a simple instinct for the removal of a physical state of discomfort due to privation, and appetite as the erotic parallel thereto, since in appetite the certain expectation of adequate gratification makes it even possible to enjoy as a kind of fore-pleasure the slight deprivation involved.   Now it is our opinion that in regard to sexuality, and especially to procreation, things are ingeniously arranged in such a way that gratification can be counted upon in any event.   Sexuality also, therefore, only *plays* with danger.   According to our description the whole sexual tension of the organism is converted, in genital sexuality, into a kind of itching of the genitalia [1] which can be got rid of extremely easily, while at the same time the regressive striving of the entire organism to return to the maternal womb is translated to one organ of the body, the genital, *via* which it can be realized without difficulty.

---

[1] Hysterical conversion would consist of the converse of this process, the transmutation of genital excitation into different bodily innervations.

The act of coitus is thus reminiscent of those melodramas in which, while there are of course dark clouds threatening all kinds of destruction, just as in a real tragedy, there is always the feeling that "everything will turn out all right".[1]

We can only imagine as the motive of such playful repetition the recollection of the once happily experienced freeing from unpleasure which Freud also has stated to be one of the motives of children's play. The fact that the human being succeeds in surviving the serious danger involved in birth, together with the pleasure derived from discovering the possibility of exist ence outside of the maternal womb—both of these remain indelibly impressed upon the mind and impel to a periodic re-creating of a similar albeit attenuated danger, for the sheer pleasure of again enjoying its conquest. It is possible that the temporary return to the maternal womb and the simultaneous playful repetition and overcoming of all the dangers inherent in the birth struggle and the life struggle of adaptation, which are experienced in coitus, act in a revivifying manner in the same sense as does the nightly regression of sleep. The periodical admission of the pleasure principle to dominance may bring solace to the struggling individual and may give him strength for further toil.

We must admit that we owe to a psychoanalytic experience our persistence in adhering to the central idea of the maternal regression trend in spite of all logical difficulties. It is extremely striking to observe with what regularity and in what a variety of mental constructs (dreams, neuroses, myths, folklore, etc.) coitus and birth are represented by the same symbol of rescue from danger; especially from water (amniotic fluid); how the sensations of swimming, floating and flying express at the same time the sensations in coitus and those of existence in the womb, and, finally, how the genital is so frequently equated

---

[1] I was glad to have come across this interpretation of erotism in Ossipow's fine work, *Tolstois Kindheitserinnerungen* (1923). He too compares the pleasure of sexual anxiety with appetite, as contrasted with serious deprivations such as hunger.

symbolically with the child.[1]   Therewith we believe we have included the whole meaning of the sex act which terminates in orgasm.   Since the libidinal tension ordinarily confined to the genital suddenly irradiates the entire organism, the organism not only shares enjoyment with the genital for the moment but shares anew the bliss of intrauterine existence.

According to the conception here presented, the procreative function thus concentrates a whole series of elements of pleasure and of anxiety into a single act: the pleasure of liberation from disturbing stimuli of instinctual origin, the pleasure of return to the maternal womb, the pleasure of happily accomplished birth; and the anxiety, on the other hand, which has been experienced in the course of birth and that which one would necessarily feel in connection with the (fantasied) return to the womb.   Since the actual return is limited to the genital and its secretion, while the rest of the body can keep itself unscathed (and takes part in the regression "hallucinatorily"), every element of anxiety is successfully eliminated in orgasm and the procreative act terminates with a feeling of complete satisfaction.

One point in our argument which undeniably remains obscure concerns the peculiar combining of the gratification of desire and the function of race-preservation in the act of coitus.   We must grant that individual ontogenesis does not provide an adequate explanation, and we must now see whether the investigation of phylogenetic parallels, carefully avoided so far, will not give us some further assistance.

[1] Should our hypothesis some day be verified, it would in turn operate to clarify the mode of origin of symbols in general.   Genuine symbols would then acquire the value of historic monuments, they would be the historical precursors of current modes of activity and memory vestiges to which one remains prone to regress physically and mentally.

PHYLOGENESIS

CHAPTER 6

THE PHYLOGENETIC PARALLEL

In order to avoid making the confession later on and to excuse beforehand our daring incursion into an alien scientific field, we should like to emphasize once and for all that the idea of seeking a kind of historical parallel to the individual experience of the catastrophe of birth and its repetition in the act of coitus was not imposed upon us by any of the facts of natural science, but only by psychoanalytic experience, in particular by observations in the sphere of symbolism. For if through observations a hundred times repeated one becomes confirmed in the preconception that in symbolic or indirect forms of expression on the part of the psyche or the body, there are preserved whole portions of buried and otherwise inaccessible history—much in the manner of hieroglyphic inscriptions from out of the prehistoric past—and if, an equal number of times, the deciphering of these symbols and characters in the history of the individual proves valid, it is perhaps understandable, and at the same time its own excuse, that one should also venture to make use of this method of cipher-reading to decode the vast secrets of the developmental history of the species. As our teacher Freud has often repeated in connection with similar attempts, it is certainly no disgrace if one goes astray in making such flights into the unknown. At the worst, one will have set up a warning signpost on the road one has traversed which will save others from similarly going wrong.

The point of departure for all the speculations which follow was, it may be stated at once, the extraordinary frequency with which, in the most varied creations of the mind, both normal and pathological, in the products of the individual and the collective psyche, both the sexual act and the intrauterine situation are expressed by the symbol of the *fish*, that is, the depiction of a fish moving or swimming in the water. Now it happened in connection with a particularly impressive observation of this kind that the fantastic idea leapt to mind as to whether, over and above the purely external similarity between the situation of the penis in the vagina, the fœtus in the uterus, and the fish in the water, there might not also be expressed in this symbolism a bit of phylogenetic recognition of our descent from aquatic vertebrates. For the human being, as our university instructors used to impress on us, is in fact really descended from the fishes, and the famous *Amphioxus lanceolatus* has the honor of being the ancestor of all the vertebrates and therefore also of the human species.

At all events, once this idea had emerged, various arguments—fanciful and quixotic enough, to be sure—presented themselves from all sides in its support. For, we reflected, what if *the entire intrauterine existence of the higher mammals were only a replica of the type of existence which characterized that aboriginal piscine period, and birth itself nothing but a recapitulation on the part of the individual of the great catastrophe which at the time of the recession of the ocean forced so many animals, and certainly our own animal ancestors, to adapt themselves to a land existence, above all to renounce gill-breathing and provide themselves with organs for the respiration of air?* And if Professor Haeckel had the courage to lay down the basic biogenetic law of the recapitulation in the stages of embryonal development of the evolutionary history of the species *(palingenesis),* why should one not go further and assume that likewise *in the development of the means of protection of the embryo* (which up to this time has been regarded as the paradigm of *cænogenesis) there is contained a bit of the history of the species, the history of the change from the* milieu *in which its embryogenetically adumbrated ancestors lived?* When we then began to turn the pages of books on animal evolution, we very soon found that a similar idea had already been expressed by the natural philosopher Oken, a contemporary of Goethe. This idea, however, was emphatically

rejected by his learned successors, especially by Haeckel himself. According to Haeckel, it is only the stages of development of the embryo itself to which value as an historical docu-
ment can be ascribed, and not the changes in the arrangements
for the protection of the germ cells, even though these likewise
exhibit a progressive development. But our conception, as
opposed to this, is that the arrangements for the protection of
the germ cells are not new creations, and so do not belong to
cænogenesis, but that on the contrary *they too represent a kind
of recapitulation*—the recapitulation, namely, of the environmental situations which have been experienced during the
development of the species. In other words, our conception
postulates that there exists a parallelism to phylogenesis, not
alone in ontogenesis, as is admitted, but similarly in the
development of the arrangements for the protection of the germ
cells—that is to say, in *perigenesis* as well; so that in this
light we may speak of an *onto-* and *phylo-* and *perigenetic*
parallelism.

It is only in the imaginative and spirited writings of Bölsche,
so well known as a popularizer and so underrated even now
as an original thinker, that there recurs again and again, albeit
expressed only in poetic images, a point of view similar to the
one here set forth. Since, however, it is our opinion, as put
forward in a recent modest psychoanalytic contribution,[1] that
such images are drawn from the depths of unconscious wisdom,
we were compelled to assume that Bölsche, in other respects
an unswerving follower and apostle of Haeckel, was in this
regard not altogether in agreement with his master. Speaking
of the male organ of copulation, he says in one place: "There
is indeed something of the past in this member. It reminds
one of the Melusina legend.[2] Man is here linked with the
fish, from which in days long gone he has descended." He

---

[1] Ferenczi, S.: *Analyse von Gleichnissen.* Int. Ztschr. f. Psa. III, 1915.
(Trans. in *Further Contributions to the Theory and Technique of Psycho-
Analysis,* London, 1926.)

[2] Melusina, a fairy of French folk-tale, was fated to change into a snake from
the waist down every Saturday night.—TRANSLATOR'S NOTE.

does not adhere long to this metaphor, to be sure, and in fact designates the question of the origin of this appendage as a problem of merely minor interest and importance—although in this we are certainly not in agreement with him. In another place, where he alludes to the fact that the salamander belongs among the first animals to pass the embryonic period in the uterus, he says, again: "The uterus became the puddle of the salamander; it passed through the gill-breathing stage entirely within the uterus"—which certainly means nothing less than the conceding of *the perigenetic supplement to the law of biogenesis* which we have postulated, or, in other words, of the analogy between the protective adaptations of the embryo and the aquatic mode of existence of the fish.

Individual observations of the symbolism of dreams and neuroses reveal a fundamental symbolic identification of the mother's body with the waters of the sea and the sea itself on the one hand, and on the other with "Mother Earth", provider of nourishment. Now such symbolism might be expressive of the fact not only that the individual lives on the mother before birth as a water-inhabiting endoparasite and then for a longer time after birth as an air-breathing ectoparasite, but also that sea and earth were actually the precursors of the mother in the development of the species, and at this stage took the place, in that they protected and nourished these animal ancestors, of the maternal protective adaptations which were acquired later. In this sense the sea symbolism of the mother would approach a more archaic, more primitive character, while the earth symbolism would pattern upon that later period in which the fish, set down on land in consequence of the recession of the ocean, was dependent upon the sources of moisture welling up from within the earth as a substitute for the water of the sea which it had lost (and which had simultaneously brought it its nourishment as well), and in a favorable environment of this kind could lead a parasitically vegetative existence, so to speak, until its metamorphosis into an amphibian was achieved. We have here a reminder of how a change in symbolic meaning may, like a change in the meaning of a word in the case of philology, contain a fragment of history—in this instance a significant fragment of the history of the species, in fact. Behind the symbolism of the plough, for example, which psychoanalysis regards as the precipitate of bygone experiences in the culture history of the race, behind the symbolism of the breaking off of the bough and the stripping off of the fruit (as in the Book of Genesis), there lies everywhere concealed the likening of the ploughed and fruitful earth to the mother. Many primitive cosmogonic myths which represent the earth as rising out of the sea include in them elements which permit such a cosmogony to be interpreted as a symbolic representation of birth; this is illustrated, with many examples, in Rank's *Inzestmotiv* (1912), and Róheim was able to provide me with many instances from the wealth of his ethnological material. And certainly the psychoanalytic day's work supplies gross examples of regression to the mother symbolism of earth or of water. In many nursery tales we have the direct transference to the earth of the love for the mother which has been renounced in the passing of the œdipus complex, acts of coitus carried out through the digging of holes in the earth, or an attempt at, as it were, total regression by creeping bodily into a hollow in the earth. Nor shall I ever forget the instance of the young homosexual with an indissoluble fixation upon his mother, who in adolescence lay on the bottom of a bathtub filled with warm water and in order to be able to maintain this archaic aquatic status or fœtal situation breathed through a long tube protruding from the water which he held in his mouth.

The interpretation of being rescued from water or of swimming in water as a representation of birth and as a representation of coitus, an interpretation given in an earlier chapter and one moreover which is current in psychoanalysis, demands therefore a phylogenetic interpretation in addition; falling into the water would again be the more archaic symbol, that of the return to the uterus, while in rescue from water the birth *motif* or that of exile to a land existence seems to be emphasized. One is also tempted to explain the various deluge myths as a reversal, of a sort familiar to psychoanalysis, of the true state of affairs. The first and foremost danger encountered by organisms which were all originally water-inhabiting was not that of inundation but of desiccation. The raising of Mount Ararat out of the waters of the flood would thus be not only a deliverance, as told in the Bible, but at the same time the original catastrophe which may have only later on been recast from the standpoint of land-dwellers. For the psychoanalyst, at all events, it is of course not difficult to recognize Ararat, the Earth, on a deeper level of its symbolism, as simply the doublet of the Ark of Noah, and both as symbolic representations of the uterus from which all the higher animals have their origin; it should only be added that this mythological material also requires a supplemental interpretation from the phylogenetic standpoint.[1]

Now we should like to ask for just such a supplemental interpretation in behalf of the explanations which have been given in preceding chapters, explanations wherein the several phenomena connected with coitus were conceived as symbolic actions in which the individual reexperiences the pleasure of intrauterine existence, the anxiety of birth, and the subsequent pleasure in surmounting this latter danger successfully. Since the individual identifies himself with the phallus inserted in the vagina and with the spermatazoa swarming into the body of the female, he also repeats symbolically the danger of death which his animal ancestors victoriously overcame in the geological cataclysm of the drying up of the sea.

So far this assumption rests only upon a simple symbolic line of reasoning. If the fish swimming in the water signifies, as in so many fertility charms, the child in the mother's womb, and if in a multiplicity of dreams we are forced to interpret the child as a symbol of the penis, the penis signification of the fish on the one hand, and on the other the fish signification of the penis, become more self-evident—in other words, the penis in coitus enacts not only *the natal and antenatal mode of exist-*

[1] Compare, further, the deliverance of the Israelites who passed dry shod through the Red Sea.

ence of the human species, but likewise the struggles of that
primal creature among its ancestors which suffered the great
catastrophe of the drying up of the sea.

Embryology and comparative zoology provide two strong
arguments in favor of this hypothesis, which at first sight certainly seems a venturesome one. The first of these is to the
effect that *the protective structures containing the amniotic
fluid and sheltering the embryo were evolved in the case of
land-dwelling species only;* the second, that among those species
in which the embryo develops *without* an amnion *no sexual
union in the strict sense takes place,* but instead, insemination
by the male and the development of the fertilized ova both
occur outside the body of the female, usually in the surrounding water. And so it is that in the fishes we find only sporadic
attempts in the direction of a mechanism for internal fertilization, while it is only with the amphibians that there begins
a continuous and uninterrupted development of an organ of
copulation, and only in certain reptiles does this acquire the
erectility which is characteristic of the Mammalia. The possession of an organ of copulation, the development within the
maternal womb, and the circumvention of the great danger
of desiccation—these three thus form an indestructible biological unity which must constitute the ultimate basis of the
symbolic identity of the womb with the sea and the earth on
the one hand, and of the male member with the child and the
fish on the other.

As against the obvious Darwinian objection that only those
species could survive which were organically adapted to a
terrestrial existence, and that the development of structures
protective of the embryo is to be ascribed to natural selection,
to the survival of a more resistant variation, we may reply that
the more psychological concept of Lamarck, which concedes a
rôle in phylogenesis to impulses and instincts as well, is nearer
to the heart of the psychoanalyst than is that of the great
English naturalist who would attribute everything to variation
alone and thus in the last analysis to chance. Furthermore,
the Darwinian conception provides no explanation of a

phenomenon observable everywhere in Nature, the return in the new product of evolution of earlier forms and modes of functioning; Darwin would probably deny the fact of regression, which psychoanalysis can under no circumstances do without. Let us therefore not be misled by this conception; let us adhere to the assumption that in genitality is to be found the expression, and perhaps even the belated abreaction, of not alone an ontogenetic but also a phylogenetic catastrophe.

CHAPTER 7

EVIDENCE FOR THE "THALASSAL REGRESSIVE TREND"

Without for a moment wishing to underestimate the difficulties in the way, we should like to run over rapidly the arguments which, we believe, favor the idea of a "thalassal regressive trend", the striving towards the aquatic mode of existence abandoned in primeval times—and in particular those arguments which make probable the continued operation in the sphere of genitality of this regressive tendency, or, better stated, this force of attraction.[1]

Let us start with the parallel which exists between the method of sexual intercourse and the structural formation of the genitalia, on the one hand, and the aquatic mode of existence followed by a land-dwelling and air-breathing manner of life on the other. "In the lower animals", we read in the Zoology of Hesse and Doflein, "in which eggs and sperm are simply discharged into the water, where fertilization then takes place, we recognize no specific behavior on the part of the individual as preceding this discharge." The higher we go along the path of evolution, however—that is, in the terms of our own conception, the more complicated the experiences which the history of the race looks back upon—the more carefully is provision made to assure to the germ cells a favorable environment. At all events, the development of external genitalia takes place quite suddenly with the revolutionary development seen in the Amphibia. The latter are still devoid of copulatory organs in the proper sense, to be sure; these make their first appearance in the Reptilia (the lizard, the turtle, the snake, the crocodile); but a kind of coitus *per cloacam*, a pressing of the male cloaca against, or its intrusion

---

[1] The word "instinct" or "impulse" or "drive" (*Trieb*) tends to emphasize rather the factor of adaptation, the purposeful element in organ activity; the expression "trend" (*Zug*) more the regressive element. I need not say that I am of the opinion, with Freud, that that which seemingly impels "forwards" obtains its energy, in the last analysis, from the force of attraction of the past.

into, that of the female, is already present in the frog. Corresponding to their double existence in the water and on land, these creatures still possess the alternative between external and internal impregnation, that is, the fertilization of the ova either in the surrounding water or in the uterus. Here too we have for the first time the development of conspicuous external sex characters, in the form, for example, of the callosities of the forward extremities in the male frog which facilitate the clasping of the female. A penetrative structure growing out of the cloaca, a penis-like appendage, although still without a lumen, is encountered for the first time in the lizard, and the first indications of erectility, as already mentioned, in the crocodile.

It is in the male salamander that there begins to develop an intimate relationship between urethral excretion and ejaculation, which first reaches its highest development, however, only with a primitive mammal, namely, the kangaroo, in which the cloaca is finally separated into intestine and urethra, and a common canal for the excretion of semen and urine, as in the human species, traverses the erectile penis.

This course of evolution exhibits a certain analogy with the phases of development of the erotic reality sense in the individual, as we attempted to describe these in an earlier place. For the at first merely groping effort of the male animal to introduce a part of its body as well as its sexual secretion into the uterus reminds us of the attempts of the child, awkward and clumsy as they are in the beginning but pursued with ever increasing energy, to obtain by force, with the help of his erotic instinctual organization, a return to the maternal womb, and to reexperience, at least in a partial and symbolic sense, and at the same time to nullify, the process of being born. This view corresponds also with Freud's conception, in accordance with which we may perceive in the curious behavior which characterizes procreation in the animal kingdom the biological antecedents both of the various ways in which infantile sexuality manifests itself and of the behavior of perverts.

At this point, however, we shall once again have to allow

our fantasies free rein if we are to arrive at even a merely provisional answer to the hitherto unsolved problem of the motive which could have actuated the amphibians and the reptiles to provide themselves with a penis—for according to our Lamarckian conception, no evolution or development occurs without some motive, nor any variation which is not an adaptation to an external disturbance. This motive may well be the striving to restore the lost mode of life in a moist *milieu* which at the same time provides a supply of nourishment; in other words, to bring about *the reestablishment of the aquatic mode of life in the form of an existence within the moist and nourishing interior of the mother's body.* In accordance with the "reversed symbolism" already met with several times, the mother would, properly, be the symbol of and partial substitute for the sea, and not the other way about. We believe, indeed, that just as the sex cells of the higher animals perish in the absence of provision for their protection, as for that matter do the offspring brought into the world without maternal protection, so every species of animal, as was actually the case with many, would have been destroyed on the occasion of the retreat of the oceans, had not accidental circumstances of a favorable nature and the regressive striving towards an ecto- and endoparasitic existence provided for their maintenance during the period of adaptation to a land existence. It was then eventually given to the higher vertebrates to effect, in the device of internal impregnation and of growth within the uterus, a happy combination of this parasitic mode of life and the thalassal regressive trend.

A further analogy between the fœtus *in utero* and aquatic animals is exhibited in their oxygen and food supply. The embryo provides for its oxygen requirement by having its chorionic villi free floating in the vascular spaces of the maternal placenta and by accomplishing its respiratory exchange by the mechanism of osmosis. *It is not the invariably functionless gill-Anlagen of the embryo itself which we would regard as a reproduction of the respiratory apparatus (gills) of aquatic animals, but, rather, these chorionic villi,* which, like the latter, derive their oxygen from a liquid medium by the mechanism of osmosis, and not, like land animals, from the air. In the placenta, therefore, the embryo possesses a parasitic organ of sucking, as it were, imitative of the gill-breathing type of respiration, which provides for the oxygen supply of the embryo (and its nourishment) until its own organs fit it for life outside the uterus, much in the manner of land animals. If we wish to take the "perigenetic parallel" seriously, we must postulate animal forerunners as living in a transitional stage between an aquatic and a land existence—animals in which the gill-breathing type of respiration was provided until they developed lungs capable of functioning. Now as a matter of fact, creatures such as these have survived to the present day, as Haeckel tells us in detail. "Midway between the true fishes and the Amphibia", he writes, "there stand the peculiar genera of *Dipneusta* and *Protopteri,* of which very few representatives are extant today, among them the American lung-fish *(Lepidosiren paradoxa)* of the Amazon area and the African mud-eel *(Protopterus annectens)* in various regions of Africa. During the summer dry season these singular creatures bury themselves in the drying mud in a nest of leaves and then breathe air by means of lungs, like amphibians. During the winter rainy season they live in streams and swamps and breathe water through gills, like fish." Haeckel then goes on to say that it is an endless matter of dispute among zoologists as to whether the lung-fish is in reality a fish or an amphibian. He himself advances the view that it constitutes a special class of vertebrates intermediate between the two, and forming a transition between them.

The further steps in the adaptation to the land existence of the amphibians are well known. In the frog there is an immature stage characterized by gill-breathing, in which, as a tadpole, it swims about in the water in the manner of a fish, whereas the adult is an air-breathing land-dweller.

We need only postulate that *in the higher mammals placental gill-breathing is limited to the embryonal period* in order to have an ascending developmental series extending from the

fish through the amphibians to man—a series in which the
striving in the direction of an aquatic mode of life is never
completely given up, even though it is reduced in the case of
the last-named species to the period of growth within the
uterus. We have only to add that this thalassal regressive
trend does not cease its activity even after birth, but manifests
itself in various expressions of eroticism (especially those of
coitus) and, as we will now add and will dwell further upon
later, in sleep and related states.

Now we cannot by any means suppose it to be a chance
variation that an amniotic sac for the protection of the delicate
embryo has come into being in those very species which at no
period of their extrauterine existence breathe with gills (reptiles, birds, mammals). In much closer accord with the psychoanalytic conception regarding the determination and motivation of all biological and mental phenomena is the supposition
that the amniotic fluid represents a sea "introjected", as it
were, into the womb of the mother—a sea in which, as the
embryologist R. Hertwig says, "the delicate and easily injured
embryo swims and executes movements like a fish in water".[1]

In train with these ideas I wish now to refer to certain
remarkable facts, and leave it to the judgment of the reader
whether we should regard them merely as insignificant
peculiarities or might count them as arguments in support of
our point of view. Referring to the development of the
chicken embryo, and in particular the amniotic sac, R. Hertwig
makes the following statement: "At the beginning of its
development the amniotic sac is small but increases gradually
in size, since it keeps pace with the growth of the embryo and
encloses a considerable volume of fluid. At the same time its
walls become contractile. In the hypoderm certain cells are
transformed into contractile fibres which from the fifth day of
incubation give rise to rhythmic movements. These move-

[1] We are also reminded of the striking changes in respiration effected in
coitus by emotion, which we have related to the dyspnœa in connection with
birth, but which we should also like now to connect with the archaic struggle
for oxygen.

ments can be made out through the unbroken shell by holding the egg against a source of bright light and using the ooscope devised by Preyer. In this way it can be established that the amnion executes contractions at the rate of about ten per minute, contractions originating at one pole and progressing to the opposite end in the manner in which the body of a worm contracts. By this means the amniotic fluid is set in motion and the embryo rocked to and fro in rhythmic fashion." It is to be noted that these movements increase up to the eighth day of incubation and then decrease, in the same way as the volume of amniotic fluid, in the case of all Amniotes, gradually decreases after an original rapid increase.

It would surprise me if this arrangement of rhythmic rocking had not been poetically compared by some naturalist or other to the surging of the sea—though in the last analysis this is more than merely a figure of speech.[1]

Even at the risk of loading down this brief work with hypotheses, we cannot suppress the opinion we have formed as to the phylogenetic parallel to the development of the male sexual character and sexual organs in their mutual relationship. In the section on Ontogenesis we spoke of an original similarly

[1] Merely in passing I will refer to the peculiar fact that the genital secretion of the female among the higher mammals and in man, the erotically stimulating effect of which, as we have said, may be traceable to infantile reminiscences, possesses a distinctly fishy odor (odor of herring brine), according to the description of all physiologists; this odor of the vagina comes from the same substance (trimethylamine) as the decomposition of fish gives rise to.

Furthermore, they may be right after all who maintain that the 28-day cycle of the female menses is to be attributed to the influence of the phases of the moon (thus in more direct fashion to the influence of the tides upon the sea-inhabiting forerunners of the higher species).

I would not overlook the opportunity in this connection to call attention also to the peculiar behavior in coitus of those mammals which after adaptation to life on land have again become aquatic animals (whales, walruses, seals). Of these it is stated that for the sex act they go up on land; in other words, they are impelled by a " geotropic " regressive trend which forces them to reestablish for their offspring the situation which they had most recently won free of. Familiar enough, moreover, is the behavior of certain marine fish which at the time of spawning swim *upstream* over great cataracts, and in the face of every obstacle ascend the mountain streams in which they themselves had their origin.

directed striving on the part of both the male and the female
to penetrate into the body of the sexual partner, and thus of
a warfare of the sexes which ended in the victory of the male
and the creating of adaptations of a consolatory character for
the female.

Now it is important to add that this warfare probably had
also a prototype in the developmental history of the species.
We have learned that even in the amphibians, in which the
organs of copulation are still very rudimentary, the male
already possesses structures for clasping the female. In ever
increasing variety and multiplicity there develop in the higher
vertebrates the means of fascinating and overpowering, where-
with the female is rendered submissive. If one takes into
consideration, in particular, the progressive development of the
male penetrative implement in the higher vertebrates (whereas
such an organ is present only exceptionally, as we have seen,
in their aquatic forerunners), one may suppose that, following
upon the danger of desiccation in which for the first time the
necessity arose for seeking a substitute for the aquatic existence
of which they had been deprived, the impulse manifested
itself, also for the first time, to penetrate into the body of
another animal, that is, to copulate with it. Originally this
warfare may have been waged by all against all; but ultimately
it was the stronger male (and the one equipped from the beginning for this rôle, as will later on be clear) that succeeded in
penetrating into the cloaca of the partner and eventually
boring a tube of its own for coitus—a situation to which the
organization of the female in turn accommodated itself.

This marked increase of sexual dimorphism in precisely those
animals that were land-dwellers, therefore subsequent to the
cataclysm of the drying of the sea, perhaps indicates, however,
that the warfare in connection with the earliest attempts at
coitus was in reality a struggle for water, for moisture, and
that in the sadistic component of the sex act this period of
struggle achieves repetition, even though but symbolically and
playfully and even though in such distant progeny of these
earliest ancestors as the human species.

The threatening and fearsome qualities of the paternal phallus, which originally represented only the child in the maternal womb, might also have their origin in this period of struggle.[1]

[1] The compelling of coitus *per cloacam* by the male would thus be the primal cause of the fact that the erotism of the female, originally equally phallic, was replaced by a cloacal "cavity-erotism" (Jekels, Federn), whereby the rôle of the penis passed over to the feces and the child. The impeding of excretion by the obstructing of the cloaca by the penis and its again becoming free of such obstruction upon the termination of coitus—thus a kind of "anal distress", as it were, and its sudden relief—may have led to pleasurable sensations in which the female was able to find a substitutive solace.

CHAPTER 8

COITUS AND FERTILIZATION

If according to our hypothesis coitus is naught else than the freeing of the individual from burdensome tension, simultaneous with the gratification of the impulse towards regression to the maternal womb and to that prototype of everything maternal, the sea, it is not so readily apparent why and in what way this gratificatory impulse, seemingly quite independent as it is of the impulse to fertilization and the preservation of the species, nevertheless coalesces with the latter and achieves expression simultaneous therewith in the genitality of the higher animals. The one point which we have so far been able to adduce in explanation of this state of things was the individual's identification of his total personality with the genital secretion. In this light the elaborate safeguarding with which the individual surrounds the genital secretion would not be any more curious than similar safeguarding measures which so many animals employ in the case of their other excretions also. It is the feeling of the individual that these excretions constitute an essential part of his very self, are part and parcel of him; and their discharge is accompanied by a feeling of loss which seems to be more intense in the case of solid matter (fæces) than upon the elimination of excretions of a thinner consistency.

This explanation, however, strikes one from the outset as quite inadequate and unsatisfying, particularly when one takes into consideration the fact that with the sexual act there are brought into temporal and spatial conjunction both the depositing of the sexual secretion in a place of safety and the process of fertilization, that is, the union of gametes of opposite sex and the inception of embryonic development. It must be conceded that the act of fertilization poses riddles of a character quite different from those with the solution of which we were concerned in connection with the act of coitus. For in truth fertilization is a far more archaic phenomenon than the temporary union of male and female in the sex act. We have seen, in fact, that the development of genitality and of its executive organ has its earliest inception in the amphibians, but propagation by fertilization, on the other hand, in the lowest unicellular organisms, in the amœba. This suggests the exact reversing of the line of thought pursued up to the present, and the inquiry whether those zoologists are not right who maintain that the sexual act *in toto* is simply a compulsion induced as it were by the sex cells which forces the individual to bring the germ cells together in the safest possible situation. The manifold precautions which are taken to this end in the animal kingdom even prior to the development of the function of sexual intercourse speak definitely in favor of this assumption, and the question is thereby raised whether this is not likely to upset our whole hypothesis of uterine and thalassal regression.

The sole means of escape from this difficulty lies in the consistent following through of the idea of the perigenetic parallel. If the life conditions of the organism in the course of ontogenesis are really a reproduction of primeval modes of life, as we have assumed to be true of the existence of the embryo in the amniotic fluid of the mother, then *there must be something in phylogenesis, also, which corresponds to the phenomenon of fertilization, and likewise to the development of the germ cells (spermato- and oogenesis).* This something can only be the unicellular form of existence of primeval times and the disturbance thereof by a primeval catastrophe which compelled these unicellular organisms to coalesce into a unit. This is also the hypothesis which Freud, in allusion to the poetic fantasy in Plato's Symposium, put forward in his Beyond the Pleasure Principle. A great catastrophe, as he terms it, split matter asunder, rent it into two halves, leaving it with an impulsion to reunion wherein organic life had its earliest inception. It would represent a not very radical modification of this idea if we were to include in it the possibility that in the sequence of fertilization and germ cell development a primeval sequence is repeated—that, therefore, living organisms have developed out of inorganic matter as at first something isolated and individual, and it was only through a second catastrophe that they were driven to reunite.   Among unicellular organisms, furthermore, there are transitional forms which stand midway between conjugating and non-conjugating types, as the amphibians between water- and land-inhabiting forms.   Thus we read that in certain of these primitive organisms an epidemic of conjugation, so to speak, breaks out under unfavorable environmental conditions, such as the *danger of desiccation,* and they begin to unite sexually.[1]   Now the fanciful Bölsche has already told us that such a union is, properly speaking, nothing but a refined sort of eating each other up on the part of the sexually conjugating organisms.   In the last analysis, therefore, the first cellular conjugation takes place in a manner entirely similar to that which we have represented in the case of the first coitus. In the earliest attempts at coitus on the part of fishes, after the recession of the oceans, it was a matter of attempting to regain in an animal body the moist and nourishment-providing habitation of the sea, now lost.   A comparable but even more archaic cataclysm may have forced the unicellular organisms, similarly, to eat each other up, in such manner that no one of the participants in the struggle succeeded in annihilating its opponent. Thus a compromise-like union may then have come about, *a kind of symbiosis,* which after a certain duration of this symbiotic relationship again regressed to the *status quo ante,* in that from the fertilized cell the original germ cells became again differentiated.   In this way a continual alternation of germ cell union (i.e., fertilization) and germ cell differentiation (i.e., spermato- and oogenesis) would be set in train.   The single difference between this possibility and that favored by Freud is that our conception discriminates in a temporal sense between the origin of life from the inorganic and the origin of the process of fertilization, whereas according to Freud these could have originated simultaneously as a consequence of the same primeval catastrophe.

---

[1] We know that such epidemics of conjugation also occur occasionally under conditions of a superabundance of food.

If, accordingly, the phenomenon of fertilization also is nothing but the repetition of a primal catastrophe of the same kind as that which we have made responsible for the origin of coitus in the animal kingdom, we perhaps need not abandon our theory of genitality after all, and may proceed with the attempt to bring it into harmony with the undeniable facts of "pregenital" biology. For this purpose it is sufficient to assume that in the act of coitus and in the simultaneous act of fertilization there are fused into a single unity not alone *the individual catastrophe of birth and the most recent catastrophe to the species, that of desiccation, but all the earlier catastrophes since life originated* as well; so that we have represented in the sensation of orgasm not only *the repose of the intrauterine state,* the tranquil existence in a more friendly environment, but also *the repose of the era before life originated,* in other words, *the deathlike repose of the inorganic world.* The mode of adjustment to the earlier catastrophe—namely, fertilization—may indeed have served as a prototype, and may have contributed towards the fusion into a single entity of the originally independent impulses to fertilization and to coitus. This prototypic impress made by fertilization upon the mode of reaction of the individual to current traumata does not exclude the assumption, however, that, from the standpoint of the individual, the residuals of tension experienced by him are simply the burdensome products, of unpleasurable character, both of contemporaneous and of ontogenetic and phylogenetic catastrophes, and as such are subject to elimination according to the laws of autotomy.[1]

The mysterious element in the fusing in a single act of the functions of coitus and of procreation disappears, therefore, if we conceive the origin of coitus in the Amphibia as *a regres-*

[1] Without going more deeply into the genetic connections which I have here attempted to establish, Freud has cast the same thought in the following words, in *The Ego and the Id* (1923): "The ejection of sexual substances in the sexual act corresponds in a certain degree with the separation of soma and germplasm. This accounts for the likeness between dying and the condition that follows complete sexual satisfaction, and for the fact that death coincides with the act of copulation in some of the lower animals." (Trans. London: Hogarth Press, 1927, p. 67.)

sion to the same mode of adjustment (union with another organism, that is) *as had proved advantageous in the case of an earlier catastrophe.*   In the light of the tendency to unification which everywhere holds sway in the psychic sphere, although no less clearly in the organic also, or in other words, the tendency to unite similarly directed processes in a single act, it is not surprising that—after some unsuccessful attempts in the lower vertebrates—there should finally be achieved a uniting of the excretion of actual waste products (i.e., urine and fæces) with the elimination of the erotic tension accumulated in the genital and also with that of *the age-old material of unpleasure* which we think of as stored in the germplasm.

At all events, this latter substance is treated with much greater care than any other excretory product.   It is also possible, however, that the greater part of the arrangements for the protection of the embryo do not represent precautions on the part of the maternal organism simply, but are rather, perhaps, at least in part, the product of the vital force inherent in the germ cells themselves—much in the manner of certain animal parasites which can make use of the originally purely defensive reactions in the body of the host (walling off with inflammatory exudate) to create for themselves a protected place of abode, usually a vesicle or pustule filled with fluid. On the other hand, we need not deny the alternative possibility, namely, that while the individual really treats this substance with greater care than he does others, this care need not emanate absolutely exclusively from love.   If our conjectures are correct, there are contained in the germplasm in rather concentrated form instinctual energies of the utmost dangerousness, which, so long as they are contained within the organism itself, so long as by virtue of their own organization they remain separated from the rest of the organism, from the soma—in other words remain, as it were, encapsulated—are accordingly unable to direct their dangerous forces against the body itself.   The care, therefore, with which they are protected is perhaps rather a care emanating from *anxiety.*   And just as it would not be astonishing that one should continue to treat with every precaution, after he had put it somewhere else, a dangerous explosive which he had been carrying carefully in his pocket, in the same way anxiety lest injury befall the germ-plasm might contribute towards its careful protection even after its separation from the body. Naturally this does not mean that the explanation of the protection of the embryo on the basis of love, that is to say, of identification, hitherto enter-tained need be relinquished, and we have emphasized it, in fact, accordingly. Every separation from the body of what-ever substance is inevitably painful, and, as we have brought out in the case of the ejaculatory act, the tension of unpleasure involved must attain a high level before the organism is willing to divest itself of the substance in question.

If one bears in mind the manner in which male and female unite sexually and in which the spermatozoa, simultaneously or after a brief and immaterial interval, fertilize the ovum, one gains the impression, in fact, that it is as though *the somata of the sexual partners imitated the behavior of the germ cells down to the smallest detail.* The spermatozoön forces its way into the micropyle of the ovum, exactly as the penis into the vagina; one would be tempted—at least so far as the actual moment of coitus is concerned—to call the body of the male simply a megasperma and that of the female a megaloön.[1] On the other hand, one comes to understand the conception, so adversely criticized, of the "animalculists", who considered the spermatozoön and the ovum as individual organisms, as animalcules. We too believe that that is what in a certain sense they are: they are *revenants* of the original primeval cells which begot them.

It is therefore as though the soma, which originally had as its task only the protecting of the germplasm, forbore, after it had discharged this first duty and thereby met the demands of the reality principle, to claim a share of enjoyment in the union of the germ cells, and developed organs of copulation.

[1] The rupture of the Graafian follicle might be compared to the act of birth—the prototype, as regards the germplasm, of the process of birth, so to speak. It is a familiar fact, moreover, that there is a demonstrable intimate (hormonal?) relationship of a permanent character between corpus luteum and uterus.

Indeed, in the biological epilogue to this work we shall have to make reference to the fact that every development pursues this course: first an adaptation to an actual and present task, then the maximum reëstablishment possible of the compulsorily abandoned original situation or status.

One must perhaps become reconciled to the idea, therefore, that, just as the unresolved and unmastered traumatic experiences in the life of the individual become concentrated in the genital and are thence conducted off, so are the memory traces of all the catastrophes of phylogenetic development accumulated in the germplasm.   Thenceforward these act in the same manner as does, according to Freud, the unresolved precipitating trauma in the case of the traumatic neurosis: that is to say, they compel to a perpetual repetition of the painful situation—cautiously and guardedly, to be sure, in a qualitatively and quantitatively extremely attenuated form—and so achieve with each separate repetition the release of a small fraction of the sum total of unpleasurable tension.   What we call heredity is perhaps, therefore, only the displacing upon posterity of the bulk of the traumatically unpleasurable experiences in question, while the germplasm, as the physical basis of heredity, represents the sum of the traumatic impressions transmitted from the past and handed on by the individual; such would therefore be the meaning of the "engram" posited by biologists. If we adhere to the view formulated by Freud of the tendency dominating all organisms to arrive at a state of absence of irritability and finally the inertness of the inorganic world (the death instinct, *Todestrieb*), we may add that in the course of the uninterrupted transmission from one generation to the next of the physical medium of the stimuli productive of trauma, the trauma itself is abreacted in each individual life, indeed in the process itself of living, to become gradually entirely exhausted, provided no fresh traumata or outright catastrophes are superimposed—a situation which would be synonymous with the extinction of the generation in question.[1]

[1] This train of thought I once (1919) communicated to Professor Steinach in Vienna, known for his transplantation experiments in animals, giving him a

The unpleasurable character of the tension discharged in fertilization would be the ultimate cause, as already stated, of the uniting of the genital with the organs of excretion; we have already referred to the fact that the impulse to castration, of universal occurrence, and expressed with particular emphasis in the psychoses, has its basis, in the last analysis, in the intolerability of this "unpleasure". The occurrence of the descent of the testicles and of the ovaries among the higher mammals might serve as the phylogenetic contribution to this conception. In the lower animals the gonads are situated deep in the retroperitoneal tissues; in the higher, they are buried in these tissues until the end of the fœtal period and only later settle into the pelvic cavity, pushing the peritoneum ahead of them. The testes descend even further, exterior to the pelvis but under the skin of the scrotum. There exist animal species (the *Talpides)* in which this descent occurs only during œstrus, and then is reversed; there are said also to be animals in which the gonads descend only on the occasion of coitus itself. In addition to the tendency to spatial proximity to the organs of excretion, that of extruding the gonads *en bloc* might also be expressed in this descent—a tendency satisfied in the end, however, with the excretion of the gonadal secretion, in the same manner as in our analysis of coitus we interpreted erection as the indication of a tendency to the total separating off of the genital, with an eventual compromise limited to the expulsion of the ejaculate.

Since it was our purpose to conjecture what might be the motives underlying the phenomena of fertilization only on the

brief memorandum in which I set forth the grounds which would justify the research worker in undertaking rejuvenation experiments. I argued therein that if, as I believe, the degeneration of the germplasm hastens the death of the soma, the implantation of fresh gonadal material would of necessity stimulate the vital energy of the soma to renewed activity, that is to say, would prolong life. Professor Steinach thereupon told me that he had already translated into practice the idea of rejuvenation by means of transplants of testicular and ovarian tissue, and showed me also photographs of rejuvenated rats. From Steinach's publications appearing shortly thereafter it was clear, however, that he regarded not the germ cells themselves but the intercellular tissue as the material stimulative of renewed life.

analogy of the comparable motives in the case of coitus, the
latter motives being accessible to us through psychological
investigation, we can hardly speak definitively on the question
whether here also, in addition to the "unpleasure" factors
which impel to fertilization, "pleasurable" repetitional tendencies do not likewise cooperate—erotic tendencies as distin-
guished from other impulses, in that they increase and accumu-
late tension for the pleasure of its release. We have, at any
rate, no grounds whatever for disregarding such a possibility.
If we once venture to assume that in the physiological process
of coitus a purely traumatic compulsion and an erotic urge
gain expression in a compromise formation, and if we do not
hesitate to ascribe to the germplasm and its cellular constituents a striving, based on motives of "unpleasure", towards
the act of fusion, we may confidently suppose that motives
of pleasure gain may here also, as in coitus, play a contribu-
tory part in this uniting. These motives of pleasure gain,
according to the point of view here set forth, not only help to
neutralize and render innocuous traumatic shocks to which no
adjustment has been made, but also celebrate the occasion of
deliverance from great jeopardy.

We have spoken of a mutual influence existing between soma
and germplasm, but we have as yet said nothing of our conception of the *influence of the soma upon the germplasm.*
Certainly no one will expect us to enter here into the highly
controversial question of the inheritance of acquired characters. What psychoanalysis is in a position to contribute to
this topic Freud has already set forth in his biological synthesis.
Besides the arguments which he has adduced against Weiss-
mann's conception of the intransmissibility to the offspring of
the effects of the experiences of the parents, we can at most cite
the psychoanalytic experience already presented in Freud's
theory of sexuality, according to which nothing takes place in
the organism which does not also have its repercussion in the
sphere of sexuality. If now sexual excitation of this kind
always affected the germplasm also, and if we might consider
the germplasm capable of registering such impressions, we

could form a conception of the manner in which an influence of the sort in question—of the soma upon the germplasm, that is—might or does arise. In contradistinction to the theory of the "pangenetic" origin of the germinal substance which Darwin taught, we believe, indeed, that the germ cells do not, as a faithful copy of the soma, merely consist of fragments of the latter, but trace back their pedigree, on the contrary, to a far older era than does the soma itself. They are, to be sure, decisively influenced by the subsequent fate of the soma—and this in an actually pangenetic sense, or, to use our neologism, amphimictically—just as, conversely, the soma seems to receive stimuli to instinctual response not only from the environment and endogenously but also from the strivings of the germplasm. Let it be borne in mind in any case that we have had to form all these complicated notions of the relations between soma and germplasm only in order to render more intelligible the analogy (and homology) between the organs and the processes of fertilization and of coitus. And possibly we have even to a certain extent succeeded in this.

To facilitate a grasp of what has been said we should like in conclusion to summarize in tabular form the "perigenetic parallel" which we have been sponsoring:

	Phylogenesis	*Onto- and Perigenesis*
I. Catastrophe	Origin of organic life	Maturation of the sex cells
II. Catastrophe	Origin of individual unicellular organisms	"Birth" of mature germ cells from the gonads
III. Catastrophe	Beginning of sexual propagation	Fertilization
	Development of marine life	Development of the embryo in the uterus
IV. Catastrophe	Recession of the ocean; adaptation to terrestrial existence	Birth
	Development of animal species with organs of copulation	Development of the primacy of the genital zone
V. Catastrophe	Ice Ages The Coming of Man	Latency period

Two rubrics in this tabulation require some elucidation. In keeping separate the originating of organic life and of the individual unicellular organism, we really postulate a duplication of the cosmic catastrophe presumed by Freud in the vivification of inorganic matter. The first of the two would have as its result only the originating of organic matter—that is, of matter constructed according to a certain plan of organization; the second, the isolating out from this matter of separate individuals endowed with autonomy and self-governance. As indeed the double meaning of the word "matter",[1] signifying literally mother-substance, indicates, we should like to regard the second process as the earliest birth of all, the model and prototype of all subsequent birth. In this sense we should therefore have to return to Freud's assumption, according to which the origin of life (at least of the individual) consisted in a disruption of matter. In the last analysis this was the earliest example of autotomy: external changes may have made the compounding of elements into a sizeable complex insupportable and have brought about their rearrangement into smaller units. Analogous forces may have been at work, indeed, in the case of the originating of the first crystalline entity, the first crystal, from a crystalline matrix, from the "mother-liquor"—the latter, moreover, by a process, once again, of "drying up".[2]

The other rubric which requires explanation is the postulation of the ice age as the most recent catastrophe which overtook the human race. In my essay on the stages of development of the reality sense (1910) I attempted to put forward the development of civilization as a reaction to this catastrophe. It is now necessary to add to this the statement that through the intervention of the ice age, furthermore, the *erotic* reality sense, which had already reached the genital stage of development, underwent a consequent restriction, and the genital

---

[1] The word in the original is *Materie;* English, *matter* (and *material*); Latin, *materia;* cf. *mater*, mother, and the Sanskrit root *ma*, make.—TRANSLATOR'S NOTE.

[2] The naive animistic mode of thinking exemplified in this conception will receive its justification in a later place.

drives, unutilized as such, were employed in the reinforcement of "higher" intellectual and moral activity.

We have several times already had occasion to depict genitality itself, in its capacity to relieve the rest of the organism of sexual drives, as an important advance in the division of labor and as a factor in the development of the reality sense. It should now be added that to this phenomenon, too, there exist phylogenetic parallels. In the vertebrates characterized by an amnion, in which, as we have learned, there develop for the first time organs of copulation, there also originates the convoluting of the hitherto smooth-surfaced brain; it is furthermore asserted that it is in the placental animals that the corpus callosum first makes its appearance, and therewith the associative connection of the two cerebral hemispheres—certainly a significant advance in intellectual efficiency. Human cultural advance in the latency period would therefore be only an expression—considerably modified, to be sure—of the age-old intimate connection between the genital impulse and intellectuality.

If, however, this is true of cerebral development, we would impart a further thought which throws a certain light on the relation between genitality and intellectuality, while at the same time pointing also to an *organic prototype* of the mode of functioning of the organ of thought. We have spoken of how significant a rôle the sense of smell plays in sexuality. We know, on the other hand, that in the development of the brain the importance of the rhinencephalon (and therewith the rôle, also, of smell in sexuality) recedes more and more into the background, while the anatomic and functional growth and increase of the cerebral hemispheres come more and more to the fore. For an organism with upright posture the eye eventually replaces the nose, even in the erotic sense; anthropoid apes and man are in very truth "eye animals", in the phrase of the naturalist, Thomas Zell. And so we believe that the functioning of the organ of smell exhibits an analogy with thought which is so intensive and complete that *smell may properly be considered the biological prototype of thought.* By means of

smell the animal tests and tastes infinitesimal particles of food
material in sniffing the volatile emanations therefrom before
deciding to consume it as food; similarly the dog sniffs the
genital of the female before entrusting the penis to her.   What,
however, is the function of the organ of thought, according to
Freud?   A testing out process, with a minimal expenditure of
energy.   And attention?   A purposive periodic searching of
the environment with the help of the sense organs whereby
very small sources of stimulation become accessible to awareness.   Organ of thought and sense of smell: both alike serve
the reality function, this including, moreover, both the egoistic
and the erotic reality function.

   We have digressed somewhat from our theme, the relation of
coitus to fertilization, but it is not easy to withstand the seduction of also contemplating now and again the perspectives
which open up before us as we occupy ourselves with the fundamental biological problem of the preservation of the species.
Nor do we claim to have presented a theory of coitus which is
unexceptionable, but we do believe, nevertheless, that it is one
which holds good in default of a better.   Did not Goethe,
indeed, say that a bad theory was better than none at all?   And
we can also call to witness Ernst Haeckel, in whose *Natürliche
Schöpfungsgeschichte* there occurs the following sentence:
"In explaining phenomena, we must assume to be true, and
accordingly retain, every theory in harmony with the actual
facts, insufficiently founded though it may be, until it is
replaced by a better one."

EPICRISIS

CHAPTER 9

COITUS AND SLEEP

"Sleep's a shell, to break and spurn!"
—Faust, Part II. [1]

To the far-reaching analogy between the strivings which are realized in coitus and in sleep we have made reference too often and too insistently to be able to retreat now from the task of examining somewhat more closely into these two biologically so significant adaptations, their resemblances and their differences. In my Stages of Development of the Reality Sense the first sleep of the newborn—to which the careful isolation, the warm swaddling by mother or nurse contribute—was described as a replica of the intrauterine state. The child, frightened, crying, shaken by the traumatic experience of birth, soon becomes lulled in this sleeping state which creates in him a feeling—on a reality basis, on the one hand, and on the other hallucinatorily, that is, illusorily—as though no such tremendous shock had occurred at all. Freud [2] has said, indeed, that strictly speaking the human being is not completely born; he is not born in the full sense, seeing that through going nightly to bed he spends half his life in, as it were, the mother's womb.

But if we have been compelled to compare sleep on the one hand, and coitus on the other, with the intrauterine state, then logically we must also compare sleep and coitus with each other. As a matter of fact, we believe that in both phenomena the same regressive goal is attained, even though in different degree and by quite different means. The sleeper, inasmuch as he hallucinatorily denies the disturbing environment in its entirety and concentrates his cathexis of physiological and psychic interests and attention upon the desire for repose, attains the goal of regression by an unreality and fantasy method almost exclu-

---

[1] Bayard Taylor's translation.

[2] Freud: *Introductory Lectures on Psychoanalysis.* London: Allen & Unwin, 1922.

sively; whereas we were obliged to assert of coitus that it attained this goal, in part in merely illusory fashion, in part in a reality sense, for the organ of copulation and the genital secretion do in very truth penetrate into the uterus. Sleep and coitus are therefore both the beginning and the end of the development towards "erotic reality" hitherto undergone. The sleeper is an autoerotic; he represents *in toto* a child who is enjoying repose inside his mother's body and who in his absolutely narcissistic absorption is altogether indifferent to the environment. The individual indulging in the sex act must make many detailed preparations, must above all secure a suitable *object,* and thus evidence a much higher degree of reality sense, before he is able in orgasm to vouchsafe to himself *in toto* the illusion of happiness similar to that which sleep provides; there are thus set for him many difficult conditions which have to be fulfilled if wish is to be translated into fact (Freud). One might also say that sleep makes use of an autoplastic technique, coitus of an alloplastic; that sleep employs a mechanism of projection, coitus of introjection. But even in coitus careful provision is made that the erotic regression shall not overstep limits such as might endanger the rest of existence; only a part of the body (the genital) is destined for gratification in a reality sense, while the rest of the body participates in the act only as an auxiliary organ and without altogether suspending the activities immediately necessary to adaptation (respiration, etc.).

Characteristic of both phenomena, sleep and coitus, is the exclusion of external stimuli, the giving up of the "life of relationships" (to use Liébeault's expression): the reduction of receptivity to stimuli, the abandoning of interest in every purpose except that which serves wish fulfilment. In respect of this characteristic both phenomena imitate, certainly, the intrauterine mode of existence, and this too with curious fidelity. Since we have already discussed this point at length in connection with coitus, we should like merely to quote the characterization of the state of sleep given by Piéron, As "caractères du sommeil" he mentions "inactivité, immobilité, relâchement du tonus musculaire, position compatible avec le relâchement, absence générale de réactivité induite, persistance de réactions réflexes, manque de réactions volontaires", and, in general, the "disparition de la plupart des rapports sensitivo-moteurs avec le milieu".

Both coitus and sleep are characterized by certain body postures which, especially in the case of the first sleep, have been described by quite unbiased observers as the "fœtal posture". The extremities are drawn up to the body, so that the whole body assumes the so to speak spheroid shape which exigencies of space made a physical necessity *in utero*. Between sleep and the embryonic state far reaching analogies can be demonstrated with regard to metabolic function. Animals are occupied in the daytime with the obtaining and digestion of food, but its absorption proper, that is, its assimilation into the tissues, takes place rather during the night, so the physiologists assert. (Qui dort dîne.) Thus sleep creates the illusion of an effortless providing with nourishment similar to that obtaining *in utero*. It is often maintained, furthermore, that growth and regeneration take place for the greater part during sleep; while growth might be said to be the sole activity of the embryo in the womb.

Respiration, the changes in which during the sex act we have already referred to, becomes notably deeper during sleep. It is possible that the diminution of the oxygen supply due to the lengthened pauses in breathing approximates in the sleeper to the apnœic state of the fœtus. Water-inhabiting mammals, such as the seal, inflate the lungs in sleep and stay under water, to come to the surface again to breathe only after a protracted interval. It is also stated of the chameleon that in sleep it inflates the lungs to a prodigious degree.

Of the plantar reflex of the sleeper it is said that it gives the so called Babinski reaction; the presence of the Babinski sign in the newborn is asserted by observers who have carried out this test on infants immediately after birth. This sign is a manifestation of the incomplete development of the pyramidal tracts, and in particular of the deficient inhibition of the spinal reflexes. But the sleeper, too, according to the statement of a famous physiologist, has only a "spinal soul". This utterance agrees very well with our contention regarding phylogenetic regression; we can assume the participation of an archaic regressive trend in the sleeping state also. (The sex act would provide an analogy to this phase only in its termination, in orgasm.)

Particularly to be noted is the innervation of the ocular muscles in sleep; the eyes are rotated outwards and upwards. The physiologists state absolutely that this is a return to the position of the eyes which obtains in animals not possessing binocular vision (as for example the fishes). The eyelids are closed in sleep, not in the manner of a ptosis, but through voluntary contraction of the muscles of the eyelid.

Further, the changes in temperature regulation which are observable in the sleeping must be mentioned here. It is a familiar fact that one becomes easily chilled during sleep and that extra care must be taken to keep a sleeping person sufficiently warm. This too would be a return to the embryonic state, in which the temperature is taken care of by the maternal *milieu*. But it is even possible that we have here to do with a deeper regression to the poikilothermia of the fishes and amphibians.

By way of strengthening the analogy with coitus, there are also "social sleeping habits" whereby two (or more) animals lie against each other in sleep for mutual warmth. Doflein describes how partridges and certain large bats sleep in a conglomerate mass, the latter forming a circle with their heads to the periphery. Many birds form dense masses of themselves in sleeping by perching on and clinging to each other; certain South American monkeys hold assemblages for the purpose of sleeping.

There also exists a certain reciprocal relation between genitality and sleep in that the periods of sleep diminish, while sexual activity increases, with maturity. "C'est par le sommeil que commence notre existence, le fétus dort presque cont:nuellement", says Buffon. The child when it comes into the world sleeps no fewer than twenty hours daily, and it is herein that his autoerotic gratification commences. In the adult ungratified genitality is often, as we know, a potent disturber of sleep: sleeplessness is often bedfellowlessness,[1] says the psychoanalyst. In old age both sleep and the genital drive are gradually intermitted, probably to allow fuller scope to the antecedently existing destructive drives.

In favor of a genetic relationship between sleep and genitality there is likewise the frequent occurrence of autoerotic, masturbatory and pollutional acts in sleep; and this is perhaps also one of the causes of enuresis nocturna. On the other hand there prevails among certain northern peoples, such as for example the Samoyeds, a kind of hibernation through the dark winter months, during which the women do not menstruate.

The close connection between sleep and hypnosis is familiar; on the other hand, psychoanalysis has had to take note of the complete identity of sexual and hypnotic relationships.[2] Psychotherapists often take advantage of a normal state of drowsiness to render their subjects compliant; and the parental command, "Go to sleep!" has a definitely hypnotic effect upon the child. Continued deliberate interference with the normal need of sleep is instrumental in many religious sects in breaking the self-will of neophytes, much as the falconer with only the aid of constant prevention of sleep induces in the bird of prey an obedience which makes it the servant, devoid of any will of its own, of its master. Clearly the desire to sleep, hallucinatorily to retire in the face of fatiguing reality into intrauterine or a still more archaic repose, is such an intense one that for its sake and in its interest all the mental and physical forces are bent to this end in an exceptional degree. It is in this

---

[1] Or, more aphoristically in the original: *Schlaflosigkeit ist meist Beischlaflosigkeit.*—TRANSLATOR'S NOTE.

[2] Ferenczi, S.: *Introjection and Transference, loc. cit.*

respect no different on the whole from the submissiveness of hypnosis, which we have had to ascribe to feelings of love and of anxiety directed to the parents ("father- and mother-hypnosis"). We have seen, furthermore, that genitality does not disdain to make use of quasi-hypnotic expedients when it is a question of gaining possession of the love object (secondary sexual characters). The cataleptic rigidity of the hypnotized subject is a vivid reminder, as Bjerre first pointed out, of the fœtal posture.[1] The question often raised as to whether love is an hypnosis, and the view we have upheld that hypnosis is love in a true sense, now finds its common answer, therefore, in the mutual relation of each of them to the mother-child situation, which needs only to be supplemented by reference to phylogenetically much older antecedents (the playing dead of animals, mimicry).

The mental state in sleep, which we have compared with that of orgasm, thus corresponds to that condition of complete gratification, free from all desire, which a higher state of organization is able to reproduce in no other way than by the reëstablishment of the intrauterine state of repose. In so far as disturbing stimuli (the "day's residue") tend to interfere with this repose, they are transformed by hallucinatory reinterpretation (the dream work) into wish fulfilments, into dreams; and the most thorough and complete interpretation of sexual dreams according to the rules of freudian dream interpretation gives as the explanation of the dream either sexual intercourse in the meaning of the œdipus fantasy, on the one hand, or on the other, existence in the maternal womb or the return thereto. Biological and psychoanalytic observations thus compel us to regard the wish-fulfilling character of dreams only as a psychic pendant to the general tendency to regress to the mother, such as is manifest in the biological world.[2]

---

[1] I cannot follow Bjerre in his other contention that suggestion is a regression to the prenatal, but must attribute this type of mental reaction to the parental influences of extrauterine life.

[2] The regression of the sleeper to an archaic mode of existence is comparable with the hallucinations of sleep, and might be termed an example of an "organic hallucination".

The analogy between sleep and coitus is still further strengthened by the periodicity which characterizes both. The accumulation of fatigue products which induces somnolence reminds one strongly of the manner in which we were forced to conceive the amphimictic accumulation and discharge of sexual tension. Compare therewith Claparède's biological theory of sleep: "Nous dormons pour ne pas être fatigués"; and the refreshing effects of sleep may have a good deal in common with the increase of efficiency after normal sexual gratification. Here too we must refer to the intrauterine state as a *tertium comparationis:* the transitory renewal of strength [1] man owes in both sex and sleep to his temporarily being plunged into that paradisiacal life in which there is no struggle for existence but only effortless growth and increase. It is asserted that in the sick the curative process goes on principally during sleep, and one speaks—rightly, we believe—of the miraculous healing power of love; in both cases Nature seems to go back to age-old generative powers and marshal these in the service of regeneration.

We would not neglect the opportunity to refer also in this connection to the pronouncements of folk wisdom and the testimony of intuitive minds which seem to support our conception. One who has had a good night's sleep feels "as though reborn". Sleep according to Shakespeare is

> "The death of each day's life, sore labour's bath,
> Balm of hurt minds, great Nature's second course,
> Chief nourisher in life's feast."
> —*Macbeth*, Act II, Sc. 1.

Trömner, a writer well versed in the physiology of sleep, in the introduction to his little book on sleep has passages abounding in metaphors to which we attach much greater significance than does the author. Of waking from sleep he says: ". . . Thus arise light and life out of the lap of night and nothingness. But the night does not dismiss its creatures for aye; it holds fast to them, and ever and again compels them

---

[1] See also Jung, C. G.: *Wandlungen und Symbole der Libido.* Jahrb. f. Psa. IV, 1912. (Trans.: *The Psychology of the Unconscious*, 1916.)

back to its silencing bosom. . . . Daily we must return again to the bosom of all-nourishing Night, in whose dark folds dwell the true nurturers of existence.''

We will quote too the lines of Hufeland (after Trömner):

> "Sleep is when the seeds are sown
> Of waxing growth—nor this alone,
> For the soul itself, perplexed and worn
> By the day's ills, is in sleep reborn." [1]

The sleeping state represents also, however, like the mental state in coitus and existence in the uterus, a repetition of long superseded modes of existence, nay, of an existence before life began. Sleep, so runs an old Latin proverb, is the brother of death. Upon waking, however, upon this daily rebirth, there go on acting those trauma-working forces which the material world has "awakened" to life. Every further step in development which necessity impels is, indeed, just such an awakening from relative repose. "Le végétal est un animal qui dort", says Buffon. But embryogenesis too is like a sleep which is disturbed only by the palingenetic repetition of the history of the species, as by a biographical dream.

The principal difference between sleep and coitus may, however, consist in this, that in sleep only the happy existence within the womb is represented, but in coitus the struggles, likewise, which the "expulsion from the Garden of Eden" brought in its train (cosmic catastrophes, birth, weaning, efforts at adjustment).

---

[1] "Schlaf ist des Menschen Pflanzenzeit,
Wo Nahrung, Wachstum bass gedeiht,
Wo selbst die Seel' vom Tag verwirrt,
Hier gleichsam neu geboren wird."

CHAPTER 10

BIOANALYTIC CONCLUSIONS

Having arrived at the end of the train of thought of which the purpose was to throw light, even if in only a provisional way, upon the meaning of the phenomenon of genitality and of its modes of expression, it is unavoidable that we should look back over the pathway we have followed and render some accounting of the methods we have used in the zealous building of our structure of hypothesis. An analysis—which could almost be called still a physiological one—of the phenomenon of ejaculation formed our quite innocuous point of departure. In connection, however, with the fuller elucidation of this phenomenon, we made use without scruple of an understanding gained from a quite different sphere of knowledge, the psychological. Whether and to what extent such a procedure is scientifically justifiable need not again be inquired into at this point. Let us be satisfied with having established the fact that this combining of psychological and biological knowledge has proved heuristically valuable in dealing with numerous difficult problems of genitality and propagation, and has furnished outlooks which orthodox science did not foreshadow.

The conception of the applicability of psychological knowledge to the solution of biological problems requires modification in a certain regard, however. It is not psychological insight of the ordinary sort, but solely and exclusively *psychoanalytic* insight, which is of help in the solution of our problems, as we will demonstrate by means of examples in the following pages. First, however, we would emphasize in the most general way that the applicability of the concepts and methods of psychoanalysis to other spheres of knowledge is a fresh proof of the fact that Freud's teaching has made accessible to our grasp a not inconsiderable portion of reality hitherto unknown to us.

At the very outset, in discussing the amphimictic mingling of anal and urethral instinct components in the ejaculatory process, we made use of the concepts, learned from the analysis of the psyche, of *displacement* and *condensation*. The detaching of specific amounts and kinds of energy from its object, its transference to other objects, or the concentration of several different kinds and quantities of energy upon one and the same object—these have hitherto been familiar to us only in the analysis of the psyche; we termed them respectively the displacement of the cathexis of energy from one idea to another, and the condensation of heterogeneous energies in a given idea; biological science has hitherto taught us nothing about such mechanisms as these. As effecting the transition to our assumption of *organic displacement and condensation* the psychoanalytic investigation of hysteria was of service, in that it demonstrated the displacement of ideational energy upon organic activity and function (conversion) and its retransference back into the psychic sphere (analytic therapy). It is to take but one further step to assume that such an exchange and interchange of energy goes forward also in the economy of the purely organic sphere and thus in the mutual relations of the organs themselves—and is accessible to analysis. And this would provide us with the first stone of the foundation of a new *bioanalytic* science such as would carry over into the field of the natural sciences in a systematic manner the knowledge gained and the technique used by psychoanalysis. We will refer presently to certain other of these foundation stones, as it were.

According to the "theory of genitality", the cooperation of organs and of their component parts does not consist simply of the automatic adding together of useful workmen to give a sum total of performance. Each organ possesses a certain "individuality"; in each and every organ there is repeated that conflict between ego- and libidinal interests which, too, we have encountered hitherto only in the analysis of *psychic individualities*. It is physiology in particular which seems hitherto to have underestimated the significance of libidinal energies in both the normal and the pathological functioning of organs, so that, even if only a part of the assumptions in connection with our theory of genitality prove sound, the *physiology and pathology of use* which has prevailed up to the present needs supplementing by a *physiology of pleasure*. Even now it is possible to sketch the broad outlines of this new discipline.

In tracing a parallel between *autotomy* and *repression* in an earlier chapter, we reversed this borrowing from psychoanalysis. The withdrawal of cathexis from unpleasantly toned ideas, of which the repressive process consists, clearly has organic prototypes; one can scarcely predict, however, to what an unexpected degree a deepening of insight in the realm of biology might result from being able, through the application thereto of the psychoanalytic point of view, to comprehend the more subtle motivations of all those remarkable vital phenomena which are based upon and attributable to an *organic repression* of this sort.

The conceptual discrimination of erotic trends which subserve only pleasure gain from other trends which subserve utility would constitute a further result of such an inquiry, and would be of general importance for the understanding of organic life. Still greater significance, however, would attach to the *tendency to regression* which governs both psychic and organic life (as Freud has already laid down in his theory of the instincts). It is as though behind the *façade* which the descriptive statements of biology supply us, there continued to exist and to operate, as the biological unconscious, so to speak, the form of activity and the mode of organization characteristic of apparently long superseded stages in the development of the individual and the species. Not only do these superseded stages function as hidden directors of organ activity as this is outwardly manifested, but under certain special conditions (such as sleep, genitality, organic disease) they dominate the vital activities with their archaic impulses in the same way as the normal consciousness is inundated by psychologic archaisms in the neuroses and psychoses. It will suffice in this connection to refer once again to the examples of sleep and the act of intercourse; in both of these the entire psychic organism, and in some degree the organic also, regresses to the antenatal and

probably likewise to a phylogenetically ancient mode of existence. In precisely the same manner we shall be obliged to
conceive of inflammation and fever, of tumor formation, and
in fact of the most ordinary pathological reactions, as the
recrudescence of embryonic and of still older types of activity.

But if this is so, and if the *meaning* of the manifest symptoms characterizing normal and organic life is concealed at a
hitherto unsuspected depth, then the analogy with the assumptions of psychoanalysis becomes even more striking, and we are
certainly compelled to supplement what has hitherto been a
more or less two-dimensional science of life with a *depth
biology*. And related to this is a point to which we have
already referred in the preceding pages. This seeing things
only in the flat, so to speak, had the result that in the natural
sciences one was satisfied, in general, with a conception of vital
phenomena limited to a single interpretation of the data. Even
psychoanalysis was not so long since committed to the view that
it was a prerogative of the psychic sphere alone that its elements, indeed one and the same element, could be inserted
simultaneously into several genetically different causal series.
Analysis expressed this fact by the concept of the *overdetermination* of every psychic act, as the direct consequence of the
polydimensional character of things psychic. Just as at least
three coördinates are necessary in order to define a point in
space, so in the same way neither a psychic datum nor, as we
indeed believe, a datum in the field of physical science is
sufficiently determined by its insertion in either a linear *chain*
of events or in a two-dimensional *nexus* thereof, unless its relationships to a *third dimension* also are established. A curious
fact, hitherto observed only in the psychic sphere, is that the
same element can be inserted simultaneously (and analytically
located) in a series consisting of contemporary events and in
one consisting of memories—thus evidencing, moreover, the
"timelessness" of unconscious memory traces. By carrying
over into biology this piece of insight gained in the psychic
sphere, it is possible for us to think of coitus and sleep as the
conducting off of current traumatic stimuli and, at the same

time, the expression of the striving to reproduce the intrauterine and thalassal situation seemingly long since transcended—
nay, we could even perceive in them a return to still more
archaic and primitive strivings towards repose (impulse towards
the inorganic state, death impulse). In the same way the
bioanalytic investigation of *all* vital phenomena would have to
uncover from under the manifest superficies the *biological
unconscious*. Thus it would be revealed that all futile questions regarding the meaning and purpose of development
would be converted automatically into questions regarding its
motives, which all have their roots in the past.

It may be possible to refer at this point to certain phenomena
to which even now this point of view may be successfully
applied. Let us take the nutrition of the infant, clearly so well
subsumed under the description of the act of sucking, the
various processes of metabolism, the distribution of the food
material to the tissues, and its inclusion in the physico-chemical
economy of the organism (calculation of caloric values, etc.).
But over and above all this it will strike the bioanalyst that the
first nutritive material of the infant is in reality the body of
the mother (or the tissue elements thereof, suspended in the
milk). On the analogy of genital and embryonic parasitism
the bioanalyst will conceive that the human being, in consum-
ing mother's milk and other animal products, is after all a life-
long parasite who incorporates the bodies of his human and
animal forebears but leaves the elaboration of this food
material itself to his hosts (mother, animal). On further pursuit of this train of thought one comes to the conclusion that
this process, which one might call *phylophagy*, prevails everywhere in the living world. The omnivorous and carnivorous
animal feeds upon the herbivorous, and to the latter leaves the
responsibility of elaborating provender out of the material of
the vegetable kingdom. The herbivore feeds upon plants,
and lets these work for it in elaborating vegetable material out
of minerals. According to the bioanalytic conception, therefore, the whole developmental history of nutrition is in a manner epitomized in sustenance by mother's milk, although repre-

sented, it is true, in a form well-nigh unrecognizable.[1]   Once attention is directed to this fact, however, it will certainly become possible to recognize more definitely in certain anomalies of nutrition—in its pathology, for example—the activation of regressive tendencies which under ordinary circumstances remain hidden.   In such fashion one would perceive behind the symptom of *vomiting* not only its manifest immediate etiology but also tendencies towards regression to an embryonic and phylogenetic primevality in which peristalsis and antiperistalsis were mediated by the same digestive tube *(Urmund)*.

Inflammatory processes have been described by Cohnheim and Stricker as being not alone a reaction to a current stimulus but a kind of tissue regression to the embryonic stage; but there are also other pathological changes which we shall understand more fully, I believe, if we recognize and describe the operation of regressive tendencies in their processes of disintegration as well as in those of repair.

Bioanalytic investigation of the phenomena of organic disease will demonstrate, I believe, that the majority of its symptoms are attributable to a redistribution of "organ libido". The organs carry on their utility functioning only so long as the organism as a whole provides also for the gratification of their libido. (Compare the libidinal functioning of the genital on behalf of the body as a whole).   If this ceases, the tendency towards self-gratification on the part of the individual organs may be revived, to the detriment of their cooperative functioning as parts of a whole—much as an ill-treated child has recourse to self-gratification.   (Compare the abandoning of utility functioning in hysterical blindness—Freud).   But localized injury, also, may result in the suspension of altruistic functioning and the instigation of "autoerotic" processes in the tissues.   When psychic causes give rise to organic disease (Groddeck, Deutsch), this is brought about through the transference of certain amounts of psychic libido to an organ-libidinal system already

---

[1] Thus the vegetable and mineral past might be reconstructed from the chemical constitution of the animal protein molecule.   The analogy between mental and chemical analysis would thereby be greatly strengthened.

in a state of preparedness. Vasomotor and trophic disorders stand on the borderline between neurotic and organic ailments—this latter classification representing in itself a purely artificial distinction. Syncope, for example, is to a superficial view simply the result of cerebral anæmia; the bioanalytic conception must add thereto that in syncope there likewise occurs a regression of the blood pressure control to a period antedating the upright posture, in which the blood supply of the brain required no such increased action of the splanchnics as the upright position demands. In syncope of psychogenic origin this regression is pressed into the service of neurotic repression.

I believe that as prototypes of bioanalytic mechanisms the structure of the neuroses and psychoses, with which we are best acquainted, will always serve. In the last analysis, therefore, it will be for an undauntedly animistic spirit to interpret the phenomena of physiology and pathology in terms of a *psychology and psychiatry of the living*—having always in mind Goethe's ominous lines:

"All forms evolve according to eternal laws,
And in the most divergent shapes is hid the archetype." [1, 2]

A not less significant, although at first blush certainly very surprising, methodological departure which we have permitted ourselves in this work has been the utilization of symbolism as a source of knowledge in the sphere of natural science. By conceiving of the "symbols" which can be analytically recognized as such in the content of the psyche—by conceiving of these as not the fortuitous and sportive expression of fantasy activity, but rather the historically significant traces of "repressed" biological situations, we arrived at fundamentally new and perhaps not wholly erroneous assumptions regarding the meaning of genitality in general and of a number of its

[1] "Alle Glieder bilden sich aus nach ew'gen Gesetzen,
   Und die seltsamste Form bewahrt im Geheimen das Urbild."
[2] Ortvay refers to the fact that the psychoanalytic doctrine of repression is capable of explaining the Mendelian phenomena of the "dominance" and "recessiveness" of unit characters.

individual manifestations. One can scarcely predict the further developments of which this point of view may be capable,
or how much unconscious wisdom lies concealed in the naïve
traditions of folklore, of *Märchen* and of myths, and in particular in the luxuriant symbolism of dreams.

The more serviceable to certain disciplines, such as technique,
was the one-sided doctrine of utility which at the present time
dominates the entire field of the natural sciences, the more it
prevented an approach to that deeper biological insight to
which no access is possible without taking into consideration,
in addition to the mechanical aspects, various pleasure mechanisms of which symbolism may be an expression.

In the analysis of genital processes we were naturally obliged
to concern ourselves in more than ordinary degree with the
question of *organic evolution and retrogression*—nay more, we
made bold to insinuate a novel theory of evolution and development in which we simply transferred to the biological sphere
psychoanalytic findings and assumptions regarding developmental processes in the psychological realm.[1] We cannot do
otherwise than sketch this attempt, at least in its essentials.

In accordance with our earlier conclusions drawn from an
investigation of the "reality sense" and with Freud's detailed
investigations of instinctual life, we proceded also in the case
of genital development from the standpoint that invariably
only an external stimulus, some exigency or catastrophe, can
have forced the organism to change the form of its activity and
its organization. In particular, and in greatest detail, we were
concerned with the adaptations effected by organic life after
one of the most recent geological catastrophes, namely, the
recession of the oceans. We said that this life adapted itself
to the new situation, it is true, but with the *arrière pensée,* so
to speak, of as quickly as possible and as often as possible
reestablishing in the new *milieu* the former state of repose.

Sleep and coitus, but especially the development of the

---

[1] Compare with this the essay on *Selektionstheorie und Lustprinzip* of the
Swiss biologist Brun, who demonstrates very prettily in the case of a species of
ant the operation of the pleasure principle in development (Ztschr. f. Psa. IX).

amnion with its amniotic liquor, and internal fertilization and intrauterine development in general—all these, according to our assumption, are nothing but arrangements for the reestablishing of that seemingly superseded period of development.[1] To what analyst would not the similarity of this process to that of psychic *repression* and the *return of the repressed* immediately occur? The similarity is so great that we must admit that as a matter of fact we have unconsciously made use of this dynamism, learned from the neuroses, to explain developmental efforts. Instead of making our excuses for so doing, however, we propose to consider this a legitimate and scientifically justifiable method, in the persuasion that the consistent adherence to this point of view can only enrich our knowledge of development. Thus we believe that the *wish* for the restoration of a compulsorily relinquished state of equilibrium never completely ceases to exist, but, temporarily put aside, is prevented of realization by a *biological censorship* which is created by contemporary ego-interests.[2] Thus there exists in the biological sphere also a modification of the pleasure principle which here again we could term the reality principle and which works in exactly the same way here as we are accustomed to observe in the psychic sphere: the same force which impels to regression operates, when it is prevented therefrom by a censorship, in a progressive sense—in the sense, that is, of adaptation and constructiveness.

The first effect of every external shock is in fact to arouse slumbering tendencies to autotomy (the death instinct) in the organism; the organic elements will not allow to go unutilized

[1] That there also exist exceptionally anamniotes which engage in coitus is surely, as regards the whole theory of genitality, the exception that proves the rule.

[2] A pretty example of the "biological censorship" is supplied by the behavior of certain hibernating animals. The temperature of the body falls progressively with the fall of temperature of the surroundings; but if the body temperature becomes reduced below a certain level, there occurs a sudden production of heat on the part of the body of the animal, the regression to poikilothermia is reversed, and the animal awakens: the spinal animal becomes again a cerebrate animal.

the opportunity for death which is thus presented to them. But if the disturbance is a far too violent one and thus results traumatically, taking place at a tempo too disproportionate to that of the organism's original creation, there occurs an incomplete "refusion" (Freud) of the organic constituents, and the elements of the beginning disintegration become the foundation stones of a further development—much as the sea-urchin eggs artificially fertilized by Jacques Loeb by means of hypotonic sea-water die off at the periphery and undergo cytolysis, but then form from the cellular elements that have died a membrane which protects against further disintegration, while under the continued operation of the traumatic stimulus the cell interior begins to proliferate.[1] The philosophical question as to how we can account for such regeneration and continued development can be answered without recourse to mystical ideas. It may be that the "altruism" therein expressed is merely the clever combination of rudimentary egoisms; but it is also entirely possible that the degree of complexity already attained acts upon the products of disintegration in the manner of a regression or at least contributes thereto, that organisms are not so eager to die but that they can and do rebuild themselves out of their own detritus—nay, utilize for this renewed development the *vis a tergo* which they received on the occasion of their partial destruction.

However this may be, the bioanalytic conception of developmental processes perceives everywhere at work only the wish or *desire for the restoration of earlier states of life or death.* Bioanalysis learned from the psychoanalytic study of hysteria that the mental power of the wish is operative in the organic sphere also, that a wish may become "materialized" in the body and may remold the body in accordance with a program of its own. We have no reason for disbelieving that such wishful strivings operate also outside the psychic and therefore in the biological unconscious; indeed, we are inclined to feel, and may boast of being in accord with Freud therein, that the

[1] The action of the sperm upon the ovum may likewise begin with a destruction, the regressive course of which is then changed into a "progressive" one.

adjuvant rôle played by the wish as a factor in evolution makes the Lamarckian theory of adaptation for the first time intelligible.

To return to our basic thesis: in the biological stratification of organisms all their earlier stages are in some manner preserved and are kept distinct from each other by resistances arising from a censorship, so that it is in the living organism that one must accomplish, with the help of an analytic type of investigation, the reconstruction of the most remote epochs of the past out of present behavior and present modes of functioning.

At all events, we have had to give up considering too complex phenomena as furnishing final explanations of development and evolution. When for example Lamarck makes the use or non-use of an organ responsible for its further development or its retrogression, he overlooks the fact that he evades the very problem in hand, the question, namely, why it is that in the living organism the use of an organ does not result in its wearing out, as in the case of an inorganic thing such as a machine, but instead of this in its strengthening. The observations made by us on hysteria and the pathoneuroses [1] make clear for the first time how, under the influence of the wish for the restoration of the equilibrium which had been disturbed, and under the importation of other cathexes, there is directed to the disordered part of the body an excessively strong countercathexis which acts on the one hand as a protection to the rest of the body against the noxa in question and on the other as a source of curative and regenerative power. This may occur likewise in the case of a chronic disturbance of function of an organ, and we should thus have in the hysterical and pathoneurotic type of reaction a prototype of the energy displacements that take place in the accomplishing of every adaptation and development.

It may be noted in passing that in the thus postulated return

---

[1] Ferenczi, S.: *Hysteria und Pathoneurosen.* Int. Psa. Bibliothek, No. 2, Vienna, 1919. Trans. in *Further Contributions to the Theory and Technique of Psycho-Analysis*, London, 1926.

of the repressed pleasure in the compulsorily accepted elements of unpleasure—introjected, indeed, as instinctual forces—there perhaps lies the true explanation of that alternation between *differentiation* and *integration* which according to Spencer governs development. Exigency imposes variations upon the organism; repressed pleasure causes the organism to regress ever and again to the status previously abandoned and to "redintegrate", so to speak, the latter.

Probably, in adaptation to a new situation which necessity has compelled, the impulse to regression asserts itself primarily in those organs and functions which through development have become "unemployed". It is, for instance, striking that in all animals with tails (dogs, cats, etc.), the caudal portion of the vertebral column, which once served as an organ of support for body segments since lost, has become an organ of gestures for the expression of emotion; these we learn from Darwin and Freud are properly to be regarded as regressions to archaic modes of reaction. It is in such lurking places, and in others of like kind, that the regressive tendency may be concealed at times of intensive adaptation, to come into play again as a formative factor when the worst of the danger has been surmounted. On the other hand, provision is also made that the most intensive adaptive activity shall be periodically interrupted by rest intervals, in which the whole organism temporarily falls back upon regression and its behavior becomes so to speak a gesture of emotional expression (sleep, coitus).[1]

---

[1] A few further "bioanalytic" considerations bearing on organic evolution and development may here be briefly listed. Adaptation may be of either an autoplastic or an alloplastic character: in the former, the physical organization itself becomes adapted to the altered conditions; in the latter, the organism strives to alter the environment in such a way that accommodation on the part of the body becomes superfluous. The alloplastic type of development is the more "intelligent"; it is the specifically "human" type, although it is also very widespread in the animal kingdom (e. g., building of nests). The changing of the environment is a far more rapid process than that of the animal's own organization; in those animal species which aspire thereto we may therefore suppose a certain "time sense" as already present. The autoplastic type of adaptation may be purely regressive in character (limitation of needs, retrogression to more primitive stages of development), but it may be progressive

Bioanalysis, the analytic science of life, will not be able to shut its eyes to the duty of taking a position on the question of the beginning and the end of life. In its inquiry into the ultimate basis of sexual attraction the theory of genitality was compelled, indeed, as we have seen, to overstep the boundaries of the living organism; Freud, moreover, perceives in the expressions of chemico-physical attraction analogues of the same Platonic Eros as binds together the world of the living. And in fact the physicist tells us that in apparently "dead" and inert matter active movement, and thus after all a more or less labile "life", prevails. The physicist speaks in an entirely theoretical sense of an actual death, of absolute rest, in saying that all the energy in the world is condemned by the Second Law of Thermodynamics to death through dissipation. There are, it is true, natural scientists [1] who tell us that the dissipated energies must be reassembled again, even though only after

---

as well (the development of new organs). The development of motility (search for a more favorable *milieu*) results in an economy respecting the accomplishing of autoplastic adaptations. (The principle of Döderlein sets forth the parallelism between "sessility" (the condition of being fixed or attached) and variability on the one hand, and "vagility" ("wanderingness") and slighter degree of variability on the other.

Adaptation may consist in the weaning from objects which provide gratification or in the accustoming to new objects; that is, in the transformation of an (at first always unpleasurable) disturbance into a gratification. This takes place through identification with the stimulus giving rise to the disturbance, and its introjection; thus from an external disturbance is created as it were a part of the ego (an instinct), and thus the world of the within (microcosmos) becomes the reflected image of the external world and its catastrophes.

Newly created organs in respect to their functions are only superposed upon the old without destroying them; even when the new functions make use of the material medium of the old, the latter organization or function, although apparently given up, remains "potential", "biologically unconscious", and may again become active under certain circumstances. Such superpositions are comparable to inhibition mechanisms: primitive undifferentiated "irritability", for example, is overlaid by reflex irritability of a specific order, and this by the psychically conditioned choice of reaction; in pathological conditions and other deviations from the normal (deep hypnosis, the behavior of the fakir), however, the psyche suspends its functioning and the organism regresses to the stage of reflex irritability or even to that of undifferentiated irritability.

[1] Nernst: *Das Weltgebäude im Lichte der neueren Forschung*, 1921.

extremely long periods of time. This conception stands somewhat in opposition to Darwin's principle of natural selection,
in accordance with which all change is ascribable to accident
only, and nothing at all is left to the workings of so to speak
immanent tendencies.[1] To us, however, who incline, as we
have said before, to Lamarck's more animistic ideas of evolution, it seems more plausible to assume that a *complete* defu-
sion of life and death instincts does not in general occur; that
there are still "germs of life" even in so called "dead" matter,
thus in inorganic matter; and accordingly, also, regressive tendencies to that higher degree of complexity from the disintegration of which they have originated. That there does not exist
an absolute life without any admixture of symptoms of death,
biology has indeed long asserted; and it is but a short while
since that Freud demonstrated the operation of the death
instinct among all living things. "The goal of all life is
death," for "lifelessness was here before life was." What if,
however, death and dying were not anything absolute, if germs
of life and regressive tendencies lay hidden even within inorganic matter, if Nietzsche were right when he said, "All inorganic matter has originated out of organic, it is dead organic
matter. Corpse and man." [2] Then we should have to drop
once and for all the question of the beginning and end of life,
and conceive the whole inorganic and organic world as a perpetual oscillating between the will to live and the will to die

[1] Once one has made up one's mind to assume that there is already somehow
foreshadowed in inorganic entities that "irritability" which we recognize as the
property of living matter, one can form an idea as to what might motivate the
attraction of these elements. The uniting of two elements into one would in
any case possess the advantage that the parts thus mutually apposed to each
other present a much smaller surface to the hostile environment than they
would if existing in isolation, whereby are provided an "economy of expenditure" and the first "pleasure". Something of this sort might even be expressed
in the act of coitus (*l'animal à deux dos*). Bölsche, moreover, incidentally compares the attraction between sun and earth with sexual attraction.

[2] Nietzsche: *Die Philosophie im trag. Zeitalter der Griechen (Entwürfe zur
Forsetzung, Anfang 1873)*. Trans. by Maximilian A. Mügge: Philosophy during
the Tragic Age of the Greeks (Notes for a Continuation), in *Early Greek
Philosophy and Other Essays*, New York, 1911.

in which an absolute hegemony on the part either of life or of death is never attained.

To us physicians the "death agony"—as indeed its name conveys—never presents a serene or peaceful countenance. Even the organism scarcely any longer capable of life usually makes its exitus with a death struggle; perhaps only in our wishful conceptions, themselves governed by the death instinct, is there such a thing as a "natural", gentle death, an untroubled and tranquil manifestation of the death instinct, for in reality it seems as though life had always to end catastrophically, even as it began, in birth, with a catastrophe. It would indeed seem as though there were discoverable in the symptoms of the death struggle regressive trends which might fashion dying in the image of birth and so render it less agonizing.[1] Immediately before the individual breathes his last, often indeed somewhat sooner, complete resignation supervenes, nay, expressions of satisfaction which proclaim the final attainment of a state of perfect rest, somewhat as in orgasm after the sexual struggle which has preceded it. Death exhibits utero-regressive trends similar to those of sleep and coitus. It is not mere chance that many primitive peoples inter their dead in a squatting or fœtal position, and the fact that in dreams and myths we find the same symbols for both death and birth cannot be a mere coincidence.

Thus we return to our starting point, the fundamental significance for the theory of genitality and, as we may now add, for biology in general, of regression to the maternal womb.

---

[1] The connection between the death throes and sexual excitement is well known. *Cf.* the ejaculation of the man who is hanged, von Hattingberg's *Angstlust*, the macabre humor expressed in so many anecdotes, etc.

CHAPTER 11

MALE AND FEMALE

Psychoanalytic Reflections on the "Theory of Genitality", and on Secondary and Tertiary Sex Differences

Against a reproach which is still frequently heard I regard myself as today reasonably proof. Of psychoanalysis it is said (although with undoubted exaggeration of the actual facts) that it would fain account for everything on the basis of sexuality. Since it is my present desire to speak of the sex differences between man and woman, it can hardly be too venturesome to speak also of sexuality in this connection, for no one can very well doubt the fact that the external appearance and the psychic characteristics of masculinity and femininity are remote effects of the functioning of the sex organs. Indeed, in the matter of establishing this fact the biologists have anticipated us. Animal experiments have shown unmistakably that the sex characters can be abolished, or even transformed into their opposites, by means of the implantation or extirpation of the gonads. Even the effects of purely psychological influences upon the sex characters are not wholly new to biology. It will suffice to cite a single example. A sexually quite atrophied male rat which from birth had been kept exclusively in the company of other males was suddenly placed in the vicinity of a cage of female rats. Within a short space the animal underwent a change in the direction of masculinity, internally, externally, and with regard to its behavior—under the influence, obviously, of the sight and smell of the female (Steinach). Certainly it is no exaggeration to speak in this case of a change in sexual character under a psychological influence; it could be demurred to only by one who rejected *in toto* the ascription of mental or quasi-mental attributes to animals.

To be sure, psychoanalysis goes further on occasion than the exponents of present-day biology. I have previously told how Freud succeeded, on the basis of purely psychoanalytic experience, in throwing light upon the most obscure chapter of biology, the problem of the instincts. His analysis of neuroses made possible the reconstruction of the beginnings of the sexual instinct in man, the demonstration of the existence of an "infantile sexuality" and of the twice occurring vivescence of sexuality, with a latency period interposed—which latter theories subsequently received physiological confirmation. It was anatomically demonstrated that in the human being the gonads are relatively well developed at the end of the fœtal period and the beginning of extrauterine life, become then relatively retarded in growth, but increase enormously in size in the prepubertal period. What we call puberty is thus not the first but in reality the second florescence of genitality; of the first, however, not the smallest suspicion existed prior to Freud's discoveries.

This success of Freud's—which did not remain an isolated one—encouraged me thereupon to take a further step and to utilize the observational data of psychoanalysis and the help of the libido theory in the explanation also of the act of copulation itself. The first of the working hypotheses which I made use of in this connection, and with which I should like to acquaint you, was that of the *"amphimixis" of erotisms,* as I termed it. I assumed that what we call genitality is a summation of instinct components, so called, and of excitations of the erotogenous zones. In the child every organ and every organ function subserves gratificatory strivings to an extensive degree. The mouth, the excretory orifices, the surface of the skin, the movements of the eyes, of the musculature, etc., are used by the child as a means of self-gratification, with reference to which no sort of organization is for a long time evident; in other words, these autoerotisms are still anarchical. Later the pleasure strivings become grouped around certain foci; the so-called oral and anal-sadistic organization evidences the beginnings of a development beyond the earlier state of anarchy. My attempt, then, was to investigate more closely the formation and development of the matured end-stage of this unifying process—that is to say, of genitality.

I became convinced that some organic prototype of repression brings it about that the organs of the body are mustered
increasingly into the service of self-preservation in such wise
that efficiency in this respect is definitely increased. The
repressed and at first free-floating libidinal strivings become
intermingled with one another (whence the term *amphimixis*=
blending or mingling), to become concentrated ultimately in a
special pleasure reservoir, the genital, whence they are periodically discharged.

Quite naturally it has been impossible for orthodox zoology,
largely dominated as it has been to the present day by a teleo-
logical conception of the sexual function as of other functions
also, and entirely remote as it has likewise been from the point
of view of an individual psychology, to be receptive to such an
idea as that which was forced upon me in my analytic study of
human individuals—the idea that the genital function is primarily a so to speak "unburdening" process, the expulsion of
tension-creating products, or, to express the matter in purely
psychological terms, the periodic repetition of a pleasure-
producing activity which need not necessarily have any regard
whatever for the preservation of the species.

The further question then presents itself as to why it is that
precisely this kind of activity should recur throughout so large
a portion of the animal kingdom in unvarying manner in the
form of coitus. To answer this question even hypothetically
we must venture somewhat afield.

You will recall, perhaps, that I felt constrained to describe
the first sleep of the newborn as a rather faithful replica of the
state of repose existing prior to birth. I added that this condition of sleep, as indeed is likewise true of every subsequent
sleep, may signify the *hallucinatory* gratification of the wish to
be in the unborn state. In the waking life of the child, gratification *via* the oral route (sucking) and later on *via* the anal
(pleasure in excretion and in the exercise of power) is destined
to serve as a substitute in the world of *reality* for the bliss of
the intrauterine state. Genitality itself is apparently a retrogression to the original striving and its gratification, which is

now attained *hallucinatorily, symbolically* and *in reality*, all
three simultaneously.   In reality it is only the germ cells which
participate afresh in the bliss of the prenatal state; the genital
organ itself adumbrates this striving symbolically in the form
of its activity; while the rest of the body shares in the happiness
of the intrauterine state only, as in the case of sleep, in the
form of hallucination.   I therefore regarded orgasm as an emotional condition accompanying this unconscious hallucination,
similar to that which the newborn infant may experience in
his first sleep or after the first appeasement of his hunger.

Whereas, then, the biological conception of the genital function has heretofore perceived only the striving for the preservation of life after the death of the individual and thus the
progressive striving for reproduction, I was forced to believe
that simultaneously therewith, and perhaps of still greater
importance from the purely subjective standpoint of the individual, a *regressive* effort, the endeavor to restore a pristine
and more elementary state of repose, is operative.

L'appétit vient en mangeant—appetite comes with eating!
After I had proceeded so far with a theory of genitality, I was
unable to resist the temptation to elaborate it further.   But I
know very well that such a piling of hypothesis upon hypothesis
is a thing not at all acceptable, or is permissible only with the
greatest circumspection.   If you are therefore right in regarding as mere vague theory what I have said up to this point, you
will have to look upon the superstructure now to be built up
on this foundation as a merely fantastic scheme.   Accordingly
I should by all odds prefer to set forth my phylogenetic theory
of genitality in the form of a kind of fairy tale.

Let me ask you to picture the surface of the earth as still
entirely enveloped in water.   All plant and animal life still
pursues its existence in an environment of sea-water.   Geologic
and atmospheric conditions are such that portions of the ocean
bed become raised above the surface of the water.   The animals
and plants thus set upon dry land must either succumb or else
adapt themselves to a land and air existence; above all, they
must become habituated to obtaining from the air, instead of

from the water, the gases necessary to their existence—oxygen and carbon dioxide. Let us consider for a moment the most highly developed among water-inhabiting creatures, our most ancient ancestors among the vertebrates, the fishes. It is altogether conceivable—in fact, biologists state it as a certainty—that there were certain fortunate fish that were not deposited upon wholly dry land but may have gone on living in shallow pools of water—a situation which offered the possibility of their adapting themselves to air-breathing—that is, of substituting lungs for the gills which had now become useless.

Now I have already informed you on an earlier occasion of my conception that strong *volition,* and not alone accidental variation or habitual practice, may play a part in the forming of a new or better adapted organ. The necessity for seeking food by moving from place to place led, conceivably, to the development of special organs of locomotion, legs and feet. It is thus that we have, therefore, a fish that hops on the ground and breathes through lungs—in other words, a frog.

Now in point of fact we have living proofs that such a description as I have given is not a mere fairy tale. The development of the frog, as though to prove to us the correctness of the theory of evolution, takes place in two sharply demarcated stages. From the fertilized frog's egg there emerges a tadpole, which like the fishes swims merrily in the water and breathes with gills. Later it develops lungs as well, and can live on land. It becomes an amphibian.

For the speculations which now follow I hold myself alone responsible. The thought that ever and again came to my mind was of the well known fact that in the overwhelming majority of aquatic animals fertilization takes place in the water and not within the protecting walls of the maternal body. Among these creatures copulation in the true sense does not occur, nor do they possess any external sexual apparatus. The female discharges the eggs into the water; the male pauses in the vicinity and fertilizes the eggs in the water. In most cases no direct contact between male and female occurs. As soon as the fish was stranded upon dry land and became an amphibian, the male developed special callosities on the thumb for holding fast to the female, and later, after it had been transformed into a reptile, evolved specific male sex organs, thus making provision that the fertilized ova safely reached the uterus of the female, there to develop. Beginning with the Reptilia, all land vertebrates pass through an intrauterine embryonal development. Mammals are differentiated from their forerunners in that their eggs are particularly delicate and have a large water content, so that they break during birth and the mother nourishes the newborn with her body fluids.

I could elaborate my theory further in relation to biological data, but I will be candid and admit that it was *psychoanalytic* experience which at this point helped me forward a step. Strangely enough, it was Freud's Interpretation of Dreams that gave me my next stimulus. In the analysis of those dreams which to all appearances have something to do with birth, and also of the dreams of pregnant women, it is very frequently the case that we cannot explain the dream image or the dream experience of the *rescue of a person from water* otherwise than as the symbolic equating of birth with rescue from water. In the dreams of people, too, who are in great difficulties or who are suffering from an anxiety state, rescue from water may occur as a wish-fulfilling deliverance. If you will recall what we have learned from Freud regarding the connection of anxiety symptoms with the first great anxiety, birth, you will perhaps be disposed to follow me in conceiving of the typical dream of rescue from the danger of drowning as the symbolic representation of the fortunate deliverance from this peril.

It was at this point that the psychoanalytic interpretation of life phenomena was again resumed. The idea occurred to me that just as sexual intercourse might, in an hallucinatory, symbolic and real manner, somehow signify regression, at least in its mode of expression, to the period of and prior to birth, so birth and antecedent existence in the amniotic fluid might themselves be an organic memory symbol of the great geological catastrophe and of the struggle to adapt to it a struggle which our phylogenetic ancestors had to survive in order to become adapted to a land and air existence. Sexual intercouse thus contains a suggestion of mnemic traces of this catastrophe which overtook both the individual and the species.

I am aware that in putting forward this hypothesis I have done something diametrically opposed to the tenets of orthodox science. For I have taken purely psychological concepts, such as repression, symbol formation and the like, and simply transferred them to organic phenomena. But I think it is not thus far quite certain whether this arbitrary jump from the psychic to the organic is really a mere aberration rather than, in fact, a happy inspiration of the sort one usually calls a discovery. I am rather inclined to believe the latter, and to see in these ideas the beginnings of a new trend of investigation. At all events, I hastened to give a name to this new method of inquiry: I called it Bioanalysis.

In the present instance my bioanalytic approach permitted me to interpret the dream phenomenon of rescue from water, with its attendant feeling of anxiety and deliverance, not only as the inherited unconscious memory trace of the birth process but also as that of the racial catastrophe of the recession of the oceans and the adaptation thereto.

The question now presents itself as to how the two sexes might have reacted to this geological trauma. It is again due to psychoanalysis that I am not left at a loss for an answer to this question. At any rate, to make myself intelligible I must first go somewhat more fully into the development of the love life of the two sexes.

It is undoubtedly true that, whereas in the beginning girls and boys are given to the enjoyment of autoerotism with equal intensity, indulging in it in the form of sucking, of anal-sadistic forms of gratification, and even of masturbation, in girls there begin very early to appear traces of *fear of conflict with boys.* We know that the human being is organically as well as psychically *bisexual,* that the boy inherits the rudiments of mammary glands and the girl a diminutive male member. This member, known in anatomy as the *clitoris,* and at the beginning relatively well developed, fails conspicuously to keep pace with the subsequent development of the body. Analysis of women shows that the zone of excitation is shifted interiorwards in the female. In the male, however, the *phallus* grows progressively and remains the leading zone of sexuality. Observations on animals show that a battle between the sexes precedes their amatory activities, in fact prefaces each individual sex act—a battle which usually ends in modesty-begotten flight and eventual capitulation to male violence. Even in the human species, wooing contains an element of battle, a phase of struggle, greatly modified though this is, to be sure, among civilized peoples. The initial sexual act is still in the human species a bloody assault which the woman instinctively opposes, only to become reconciled to it ultimately and even to find satisfaction and happiness in it.

As an adherent of Haeckel's recapitulation theory, according to which the developmental history of the individual is an abbreviated repetition of the developmental history of the species, I formulated the following conception of the relations of the sexes in the course of adaptation to a land existence:

There probably awoke in both sexes the striving to furnish within the interior of a food- and moisture-providing organism a shelter for the germ cells, as a substitute for the *loss of the aquatic mode of life*, and at the same time the desire to share with the germ cells this fortunate state, at least symbolically and hallucinatorily. Both, accordingly, developed the male sexual organ, and there came about, perhaps, a tremendous struggle, the outcome of which was to decide upon which sex should fall the pains and duties of motherhood and the passive endurance of genitality. In this struggle the female sex succumbed, yet gained its compensation in understanding how to fashion out of suffering and affliction the happiness of womanhood and motherhood. I will return later to the importance of this achievement and its psychological consequences, and will only remark here that this phenomenon—supposing it to exist—not only helps to explain *the greater physiological and psychological complexity of the female,* but puts woman, at least organically speaking, in the light of a more *finely differ-*

entiated being, that is, one adapted to more complex situations.
The male has imposed his will upon the female, and in so doing
has spared himself the task of adaptation; he has remained the
more primitive. The female on the other hand knew how to
adapt herself not only to the difficulties in the environment but
to the brutality of the male.

But humiliation was to overtake the male sex, too, and it was
again a geological catastrophe which, at least in my opinion,
may have given the external impetus thereto. I have in mind
the era of the renewed covering of large portions of the surface
of the earth with ice and water, the successive ice ages. Some
of the creatures affected by this calamity attempted to adapt
to it "autoplastically"—that is, by developing coverings for the
maintenance of warmth; others, in particular the animal forerunners of man and perhaps even aboriginal man himself,
rescued themselves through a further development of the brain
and the creation of a civilization which should insure preservation even under difficult conditions.

And here is the place, at least by way of a suggestion in passing, to make reference to a great discovery at which Freud
arrived on the basis of the psychoanalytic point of view, sup-
ported by the prior assumptions of Darwin and Robertson
Smith. I have already mentioned the importance of the
so-called œdipus complex in the development of every individual, its directing influence upon the traits of character of
the healthy and upon the symptoms of those who develop
neurotic illness. The mischievous revolt of the son against
the father, for the purpose of obtaining possession of the
mother and of women, ended in a complete fiasco; none of the
sons was strong enough, as the father once had been, to impose
his will on the whole clan, and a bad conscience forced them to
long to return to, and to reestablish, the authority of the father
and respect for the mother. In the individual this struggle is
repeated with the same outcome; the puberty of earliest childhood is followed by a long latency period which, according to
my view, possibly repeats in the life of the individual the
adaptive struggle of the ice age or its outcome in the creation
of human civilization.

There now arises the question whether observation of the behavior of human beings and animals furnishes any arguments for the credibility of these seemingly fantastic suppositions. Psychoanalysis speaks of the "prototypicality of sexuality". It maintains that the sex of the individual and the direction which its development takes influence decisively the trends of the total personality. The man who is free in his sexuality is bold and resolute in his other undertakings; it is not for nothing that the legend represents Don Juan not only as a successful payer of court but as a skilful and courageous swordsman who has much spilt blood on his conscience. This aggressivity, however attenuated by the humiliation incident to the œdipus conflict with the father (castration anxiety), characterizes the male psyche in general. Whereas to the woman there is left only beauty as a weapon, she is characterized in addition by kindness and modesty. These and similar traits of character might as *tertiary sex characters* be set alongside the secondary, which refer to organic sex characteristics. Among these latter I might mention in the male, in addition to his aggressive sexual apparatus, his greater physical strength and the relatively greater development of the brain. The history of sexual differentiation in the individual life-cycle I can therefore utilize in a general way in support of this theory of mine of a phase of struggle.

Obviously the old question will here occur to many as to which of the two sexes is superior or inferior. I believe that this question cannot be answered unequivocally by the psychoanalyst. I have already said that I considered the female organism more finely differentiated, and one could therefore consider it more highly developed. Woman is innately wiser and better than man; as offset to this, man has to keep his brutality in check by a more marked development of the intelligence and of the moral superego. Woman is a creature of finer feelings (moral) and of finer sensibility (æsthetic), and has more "common sense"; but man created, perhaps as a measure of protection against his own greater primitiveness, the strict rules of logic, ethics and æsthetics which woman in her awareness of an inner trustworthiness in all such things makes light of or disregards.

I think, however, that the organic adaptation of woman is no less admirable than the psychological of man.

This statement of the matter does not at all exclude the possibility of there being instances in which the intelligence of the woman far exceeds the average analogous accomplishment of the man. Indeed, the tendency on the part of many women to engage in "masculine" activities proves not infrequently to be neurotically conditioned. According to the most recent investigations of Freud the so-called "masculinity complex" is the nuclear complex in the majority of the neuroses of women and the major cause of frigidity. I would add that at the same time it indicates regression to the phase of struggle for sexual differentiation not only in childhood but in connection as well with the catastrophe of the drying up of the sea. Many neurotic women are unable to give up their symptoms as long as they are incapable of reconciling themselves to the fact of not having been born a man (penis envy), just as neurotic men have to bring to a successful issue in the analysis their unsuccessful resolution of the œdipus situation.

I have already spoken of my conception of suggestion and hypnosis. Fright and seduction I regard as the two means of rendering another person tractable. I have called these father-hypnosis and mother-hypnosis respectively. One may describe the state of falling in love as a mutual hypnotization in which each sex brings its own weapons to bear—the man primarily his physical, intellectual and moral strength with which he impresses his inamorata, the woman her beauty and other merits which make her the ruler over even the so-called stronger sex. In the sleep-like state of consciousness of orgasm this battle of the sexes finds a temporary respite, and both the man and the woman enjoy for a brief moment the happiness of an infantility free equally from desire and from struggle.

In old age sex differences become effaced to some extent. Apparently in consequence of the atrophy of gonadal function the voice of woman becomes somewhat harsher and there is occasionally even a tendency toward the growth of a mustache. But man, too, loses much of his masculine appearance and character; so that one may say that in both sexes their fundamental bisexuality is more transparent in childhood and old age.

It lies in the nature of things that woman, to whom motherhood is so much more significant than fatherhood is to man, should be somewhat less disposed to polygamy. The classification of women favored by many into a maternal type and, on the other hand, one which pays homage predominantly to love, is only a mark—according to the observations of psychoanalysis—of the sharp distinction demanded by civilization between *tenderness* and *sensuality*. This demand, when made with excessive strictness, renders it difficult for the man as well to effect the normal fusion of these two impulses in married love.

With a view to giving further homogeneity to this train of thought, I must refer to certain results in the field of psychoanalytic ethnology. Almost all primitive peoples follow out certain customs which cannot be explained otherwise than as a survival of an emasculation or castration rite practised at some time or other. The last survival of this rite, one prevailing even today, is circumcision. It is more than probable that this punishment, or the threat thereof, was the major weapon of the father against the sons in aboriginal times. The subjection of the son to the punitive power of the father, and the giving up of a part of sexual brutality, is the consequence of the so-called castration complex. If you will recall what I said earlier regarding the significance of the genital as a reservoir of pleasure, it will perhaps not seem to you impossible of belief that the masculinity and castration complex should play such a surpassing rôle in the development of the sex characters, nor that fixation at any stage prior to the resolution of these complexes, or regression to such a stage, should underlie all the neuroses.

In the light of the considerations here briefly resumed, the male member and its function appears as the *organic symbol* of the restoration—albeit only partial—of the fœtal-infantile state of union with the mother and at the same time with the geological prototype thereof, existence in the sea.

INDEX

Aggressiveness, in the male, 105
Amniotic fluid, development of, 50
  as "a sea introjected", 56
  embryo rocked in, 57
Amphimixis, of erotisms, 5–14, 97–98
  and coitus, 15–19
Apes and man, as "eye animals", 69

Babinski reaction, in sleep, 75–76
"Biological censorship", and ego-interests, 89
Bisexuality, of human beings, 102–103
Bjerre, on cataleptic rigidity and fœtal posture, 78
  on suggestion, 78n
Bölsche, on sexual union, 62

Cænogenesis, and development of protection of the embryo, 45–46
Claparède, on sleep, 79
Coitus, Freud's conception of, 56
  and sleep, 56, 73–80
  and fertilization, 60–72
  origin of, 63–64
  and external stimuli, 74
  and body posture, 74, 75
  and respiration, 75
  and changes in temperature, 76
  and hypnosis, 77
  and existence before life began, 80
  and struggle, 80
Conjugation, epidemic of, 62
  a form of eating each other up, 62

Darwin, Charles, on theory of pangenetic origin, 69
"Day's residue", and wish fulfilment, 78
Death, hastened by degeneration of germplasm, 68
  utero-regressive trends in, 95
Deluge myths, reversal of facts in, 50
Dreams, wish fulfilment and regressions in, 78

Falling in love, as mutual hypnotization, 106
Fertilization, and origin of coitus, 63
  and "unpleasure" factors, 68
  and pleasure, 68
Fish, symbolic meaning of, 45
  and Melusina legend, 46
  child in mother's womb as, 50
  and embryo's movements, 56

Freud, Sigm., on coitus, 53
  on origin of life, 62
  case of traumatic neurosis, 66
  on inheritance of acquired characters, 68
  on theory of sexuality, 68
  on organ of thought, 70
  on œdipus complex, 104
  on "masculinity complex", 106

Genitality, and hypnosis, 78
  phylogenetic theory of, 44–72, 99–102, 103–104, 105
  nature of, 97, 98–99
Genital secretion, identification with, 60
Germplasm, death hastened by degeneration of, 68

Haeckel, recapitulation theory of, 45–46, 103
Hibernation, and menstruation, 77
Hypnosis, and sleep, 77–78

Inheritance, of acquired characters, 68

Lamarckian theory of evolution, and bioanalysis, 90–91, 94
Life, Freud's conception of origin of, 62
  and death, 93–95
Love, and hypnosis, 78

Male and female, differentiation between, 102–104, 105–106
Menstruation, interrupted by hibernation, 177
Mother, and the sea, 48
  case of homosexual, 48
  origin of word for and root of, 70

Nursery tales, œdipus complex in, 48
Nutrition, developmental history of, 85–86

Odor, stimulating effect of, 57
Œdipus complex, in individual development, 104, 105
Oken, on cænogenesis, 45
Old age, sex differences in, 106–107
Organic disease, attributable to redistribution of "organ libido", 86
Organic life, impulse to reunion in, 61
"Organ libido", and organic disease, 86
Orgasm, nature of, 99